Soccer:

A Step-by-Step Guide on How to Score, Dribble Past the Other Team, and Work with Your Teammates

Dylan Joseph

Soccer:
A Step-by-Step Guide on How to Score, Dribble Past the
Other Team, and Work with Your Teammates
By: Dylan Joseph

Bonus!

Wouldn't it be nice to have the steps in this book on an easy 3-page printout for you to take to the field? Well, here is your chance!

Go to this Link for an **Instant** 3-Page Printout:
UnderstandSoccer.com/free-printout

This FREE guide is simply a "Thank You" for purchasing this book. This 3-page printout will ensure that the knowledge you obtain from this book makes it to the field.

Table of Contents

About the Author

There I was, a soccer player who had difficulties scoring. I wanted to be the best on the field but lacked the confidence and know-how to make my goal a reality. Every day, I dreamed about improving, but the average coaching and my lack of knowledge only left me feeling alone and like I couldn't attain my goal. I was a quiet player and my performance went unnoticed.

This all changed after my junior year on the Varsity soccer team of one of the largest high schools in the state. During the team and parent banquet at the end of the season, my coach decided to say something nice about each player. When it came to my turn to receive praise, the only thing he came up with was that I had scored two goals that season even though it was against a lousy team, so they didn't really count...

It was a very painful statement that after the 20+ game season, all that could be said of my efforts were two goals that didn't count. Since that moment, I have been forever changed considering one of my greatest fears came true; I was called out in front of my family and friends. Because of that, I got serious. With a new soccer mentor, I focused on the training to obtain the skills to build my confidence and become the goal scorer I always dreamed of being. The next season I moved up to the starting position of center midfielder and scored my first goal of the 26 game season in only the third game.

I kept up the additional training led by a proven goal scorer to build my knowledge. Fast forward to present day and as a result of the work and focus on the necessary skills, I figured out how to become a goal scorer who averages about two goals and an assist per game, all because of an increase in my understanding of how to play soccer. I was able to take my game from bench-warmer who got called out in front of everybody to the most confident player on the field.

Currently, I am a soccer trainer in Michigan working for Next Level Training. I advanced through their rigorous program as a soccer player and was hired as a trainer. This program has allowed me to guide world-class soccer players for over a decade. I train soccer players in formats ranging from one-hour classes to weeklong camps and from instructing groups of 30 soccer players all the way down to working one-on-one with individuals looking to play for the United States National Team. If you live in the Metro Detroit and want to be the best player in the league, Next Level Training is for you. Learn more at www.next-leveltraining.com.

Additional Books by the Author that are Available on Amazon:

Soccer Training: A Step-by-Step Guide on 14 Topics for Intelligent Soccer Players, Coaches, and Parents

Soccer Defending: A Step-by-Step Guide on How to Stop the Other Team

Preface

Soccer Shooting & Finishing dives deep into the different ways you can strike the ball, as well as the common scenarios that a soccer player will find themselves in during a game, such as a 1v1, 2v1, 1v2, and 2v2. Though the correct form and tactics are extremely helpful in ensuring the ball ends up in the opponent's net, you also need a strong mindset to improve on any weaknesses, solidify your strengths, and implement many tips, tricks, tweaks, and techniques to become the person on your team that consistently scores.

Soccer Dribbling & Foot Skills discusses how average soccer players pass the ball as soon as they receive it, but great soccer players are able to dribble past a defender or two if that is what is needed to help their team score. This book dives deep into how to dribble the ball properly and the different foot skills to use to dribble past the other team. Though the correct form and tactics are helpful in ensuring the ball ends up in the opponent's net, you also need a solid understanding of what skills to use in which situations.

Soccer Passing & Receiving talks about how underperforming soccer players consider a pass that travels to their teammate a success. Great soccer players know where to pass the ball to make it as easy for their teammate as possible. This book dives deep into how to pass the ball correctly and the keys to receive the ball with ease. This book gives you the tips, tricks, tweaks, and techniques to become the person on your team that can consistently pass around the other team.

This book will help you become the most admired player on your team. Understand that changing up one or two things may help you become better, but once you start implementing most, if not all of the techniques described in this book, you will see a significant improvement in your performance on the field. The knowledge in this book is only helpful when applied. Therefore, apply it to be sure you are scoring 10X more goals each season, which will lead to several more wins every season for your team. For any words that you are unsure of the meaning, please reference the glossary in the back of the book.

INDIVIDUAL SOCCER PLAYER'S PYRAMID

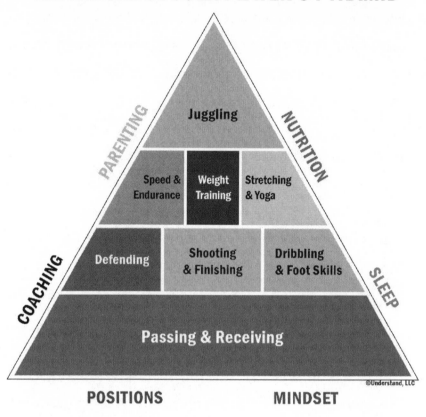

If you are looking to improve your skills, your child's confidence, or your players' abilities, it is essential to understand where this book fits into the bigger picture of developing a soccer player. In the image above, you can see that the most critical field-specific things to work on are at the base of the Individual Soccer Player's Pyramid. Note: A team's pyramid may look slightly different based on the tactics the players can handle and the approach the coach decides to use for games. The pyramid is a quality outline when you are looking to improve an individual soccer player's game. All of the elements in the pyramid and the items surrounding it play a meaningful part in becoming a better player, but certain things should be read and mastered first before moving on to other topics.

You will notice that passing & receiving is at the foundation of the pyramid because if you can receive a pass and make a pass in soccer, you will be a useful teammate. Though you may not be the one that is consistently scoring, the person that is dispossessing the other team, or the player that can dribble through several opponents, you will have the fundamental tools needed to play the sport and contribute to your team.

As you move one layer up, you find yourself with a decision to make on how to progress. Specifically, the pyramid is created with you in mind because each soccer player and each soccer position has different needs. Therefore, your choice regarding which path to take first is dictated by the position you play and more importantly, by the position that you want to play. In soccer and life, just because you are in a particular spot, position, or even a job, it does not mean that you have to stay there forever if that is not your choice. However, it is not recommended to refuse playing a position if you are not in the exact role you want. It takes time to develop the skills that will allow you to make a shift from one position to another.

If you are a forward or if you want to become one, then consider your route on the second layer of the pyramid to start with shooting & finishing. As your abilities to shoot increase, your coach will notice your new finishing skills and be more likely to move you up the field if you are not a forward already. Be sure to communicate to the coach that you desire to be moved up the field to a more offensive position, which will increase your chances as well. If you are already a forward, then dive deep into this topic to ensure you become the leading scorer on your team and in the entire league. Notice that shooting & finishing is considered less critical than passing & receiving because you have to pass the ball up the field before you can take a shot on net.

Otherwise, you can start by progressing to dribbling & foot skills from passing & receiving because the proper technique is crucial to dribble the ball well. It is often necessary for a soccer player to use a skill to protect the ball from the other team or to advance the ball up the field to place their team in a favorable situation to score. The selection of this route is often taken first by midfielders and occasionally by forwards.

Defending is another option of how you can proceed from passing & receiving. Being able to keep the other team off the scoreboard is not an easy task. Developing a defender's mindset, learning which way to push a forward, understanding how to position your body, knowing when to foul, and using the correct form for headers is critical to a defender on the back line looking to prevent goals.

Finish all three areas in the second layer of the pyramid before progressing up the pyramid. Dribbling and defending the ball (not just shooting) are useful for an attacker, shooting and defending (not just dribbling) are helpful for a midfielder, while shooting and dribbling (not just defending) are helpful for a defender. Having a well-rounded knowledge of the skills needed for the different positions is important for all soccer players. It is especially essential for those soccer players looking to change positions in the future. Shooting & finishing, dribbling & foot skills, and defending are oftentimes more beneficial for soccer players to learn first than the next tier of the pyramid, so focus on these before spending time on areas higher up in the pyramid. In addition, reading about each of these areas will help you to understand what your opponent wants to do as well.

Once you have improved your skills at the 1st and 2nd tiers of the pyramid, move upwards to fitness. As you practice everything below this category on the pyramid, your fitness and strength will naturally increase. It is difficult to go through a passing/dribbling/finishing drill for a few minutes without being out of breath. Performing the technical drills allows soccer players to increase their fitness naturally. This reduces the need to focus exclusively on running for fitness. Coming from a soccer player and trainer (someone with a view from both sides), I know that a constant focus on running is not as fulfilling and does not create long-lasting improvements. Whereas, emphasizing the shooting capabilities, foot skills, and defending knowledge of a soccer player does create long-lasting change. Often, the coaches that focus on running their players in practice are the coaches that care to improve their team but have limited knowledge of many of the soccer-specific topics that would quickly increase their players' abilities. Not only does fitness in soccer include your endurance, but it also addresses your ability to run with agility and speed, develop strength and power, while improving your flexibility through stretching and yoga to become a well-rounded soccer player.

Similarly to the tier below it, you should focus on the fitness areas that will help you specifically, while keeping all of the topics in mind. For example, you may be a smaller soccer player that could use some size. Then, you would emphasize weight training and gain the muscle to avoid being pushed off the ball. However, you would still want to stretch before and after a lifting workout or soccer practice/game to ensure that you stay limber and flexible, so that you can recover quickly and avoid injuries.

Maybe you are a soccer player in your 20s, 30s, or 40s. Then, emphasizing your flexibility and practicing a bit of yoga would do a world of good to ensure you keep playing soccer for many more years. However, doing a few sets of push-ups, pull-ups, squats, lunges, sit-ups, etc. per week will help you maintain or gain a desirable physique.

Furthermore, you could be in the prime of your career in high school, college, or at a pro level, which would mean that obtaining the speed and endurance to run for 90+ minutes is the most essential key to continue pursuing your soccer aspirations.

Finally, we travel to the top of the pyramid, which includes juggling. Juggling the soccer ball is something fun to practice in your own free time away from the field or when you are standing in line and waiting to start a drill. It will certainly help with your first touch, but there are more important things to develop during an individual's or team's practice. A general recommendation is that when you can juggle the ball 50 times in a row or more with either of your feet, continuing to work on juggling will not provide huge increases in your performance. Therefore, use juggling as a way to fill otherwise unproductive time in training or during free time to more quickly become a great soccer player. The importance of juggling is explained in more detail in the first book of the series - Soccer Training: A Step-by-Step Guide on 14 Topics for Intelligent Soccer Players, Coaches, and Parents, in addition to a host of other critical topics you need to know as a soccer player, coach, or parent.

If you have not read Soccer Training: A Step-by-Step Guide, it is highly recommended that you do to gain general knowledge of the crucial topics within the areas of the pyramid. Furthermore, there are a few soccer terms that are described in detail in the Soccer Training book that may only be referenced in this book. Picking up a copy of the book will act as a good gauge to see how much you know about each topic. This will help to determine if a book later in the series written about a specific subject in the soccer pyramid will be beneficial for you.

The last portion of the pyramid are the areas that surround the pyramid. Though these are not skills and topics that can be addressed by your physical abilities, they each play key roles in rounding out a complete soccer player. For example, having a supportive parent/guardian or two is beneficial for transporting the child to games, providing the equipment needed, the fees for the team, expenses for individual training, and encouragement. Having a quality coach will help the individual learn how their performance and skills fit into the team's big picture.

Sleeping enough is critical to having energy in practices and on game days, in addition to recovering from training and games. Appropriate soccer nutrition will increase the energy and endurance of a soccer player, help the soccer player achieve the ideal physique, and significantly aid in the recovery of the athlete. Understanding soccer positions will help to determine if a specific role is well-suited given your skills. It is important to know that there are additional types of specific positions, not just forwards, midfielders, and defenders. A former or current professional player in the same position as yours can provide you guidance on the requirements of effectively playing that position. Last, but not least, is developing a mindset that leaves you unshakable. This mindset will help you become prepared for game situations, learn how to deal with other players, and be mentally tough enough to not worry about circumstances that you cannot control, such as the type of field you play on, the officiating, or the weather. The pyramid is a great visual aid to consider when choosing what areas to read next as a soccer player, coach, or parent. Now that you know where each of these three books play into the bigger picture, let us begin.

Soccer Shooting & Finishing:

A Step-by-Step Guide on How to Score

Chapter 1

1v1s

A soccer player that can go up against one defender and win at least 80% of the time is very rare in soccer. These players are coveted by coaches because they know that this player will be able to create space away from the opposition to take more shots on net. **More shots generally mean a much higher probability for goals or rebounds that turn into goals.** Please understand that you still want to make good decisions and avoid taking low probability shots or dribbles just to take unreasonable shots. **Therefore, as a soccer player developing your skills to perform in 1v1 situations successfully, consider the following three things:**

1. Use a foot skill.
2. Attack with speed.
3. Aim to use your dominant foot to shoot.

First, use a foot skill!!! Using a foot skill to create space is one piece of advice that should most definitely be followed in a 1v1 situation, but sadly few players actually do. Most wait to pass the ball to a supporting teammate or try to outrun the opposition by kicking the ball past the defender and using his or her speed. Specifically, use a jab step or a scissor to fake as if you are going to your weak foot. Done correctly, this will enable you to have created a foot or two of space to explode forward with your dominant foot. An attacking skill where the defender is backpedaling often lures the defender to commit to going in the wrong direction. If the defender goes the wrong way, he or she will be off balance, which significantly increases the chance for you to shoot without your shot being blocked or even for you to travel entirely past the defender, allowing you a one-on-one opportunity with the opponent's goalie.

Next, attack with speed. A 1v1 situation is excellent for a forward that usually has two or three defenders covering them. Attack as if you do not have any support coming, but do not be afraid to make a pass if you see a teammate out of the corner of your eye. You cannot be looking straight down at the ball when dribbling. Instead, you should be looking five or so yards past the ball to see a teammate or potentially another defender. In addition, occasionally take a quick glance to see where the goalkeeper is because, in 1v1 situations, goalies will often come further out of their net which may present you an excellent opportunity to chip the ball over them.

Goalies will often creep up the field and out of their net because they realize that a forward is trained to beat a defender and has a pretty good chance of winning the 1v1 battle against the defender. This frees the attacker to have a shot or dribble towards the net, so the goalie will want to come out a little bit to cut down the angle of the shot. If the goalkeeper is standing square in the middle of the net when the striker shoots, there is very little chance that they will save shots that are close to either of the posts. However, if the goalie comes out and cuts the angle off, they are limiting the amount of net into which the striker can shoot. **The speed after the skill is critical to create the space and separation between you and the defender.** Jog by the defender and they will sprint to catch up. Sprint by the defender and you will most likely not have to beat them again on that specific attempt to score.

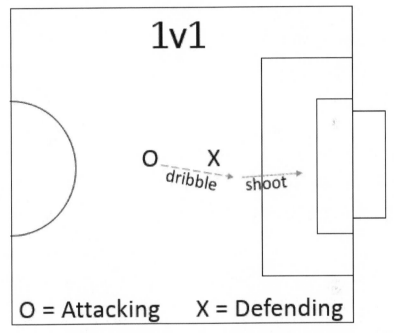

Lastly, whenever you have a 1v1 situation while attacking towards the other team's net, your goal should be to take your shot with your dominant foot. **Obviously, the foot that you are more comfortable using will provide a more accurate and powerful shot on target compared to a shot with your opposite foot.** In a 1v1, because only one person is defending you, a good striker should be able to go in the direction that he or she wants. Therefore, if you are right-footed, practice those left-footed jab steps and scissors to ensure that the ball ends up on your right foot when you go to shoot.

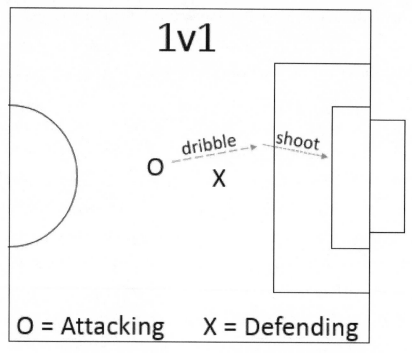

However, you do not want to go to your dominant foot 100% of the time because, on occasion, the defender will be letting you go to your weak foot by completely cutting off your path up the field towards your dominant foot. **In a situation where the defender gives you a lot of space to your weak foot, take it because you will be able to push well past the defender to ensure that you can take a shot with your opposite foot.** Since you will have much more space than going to your dominant foot, it will be easier for you to take a powerful and well-driven shot on target when you go to strike the ball. Otherwise, use a jab step, scissor, or inside of the foot shot fake to help create space to enable you to travel to your dominant foot. Also, consider if you have gone against that defender already in the game. Use the information on what makes your opponent uncomfortable, what worked, and what you think may work to increase your chance of beating them.

To conclude, your objectives when attacking in a 1v1 are to use a skill to create space, attack with speed to take the space that the foot skill created, and more often than not, use a foot skill that will place the ball on your dominant foot when you go to strike the ball. Capitalize on 1v1s to ensure you score a goal for your team and build your confidence as a soccer player. This chapter may also be found in the next book in the Understand Soccer Series – *Soccer Dribbling & Foot Skills: A Step-by-Step Guide on How to Dribble Past the Other Team.* 1v1s are related to dribbling and foot skills as much as they are related to shooting and finishing. If you found this chapter helpful, pick up the Soccer Shooting & Finishing Book for chapters on 2v1s, 1v2s, and 2v2s, among varying other topics.

Chapter 2

Shooting a Driven Shot

This chapter has been extracted from the first book in the Series - *Soccer Training: A Step-by-Step Guide on 14 Topics for Intelligent Soccer Players, Coaches, and Parents*. The first book in the Understand Soccer series is recommended for grasping overall knowledge in the key areas of soccer. Even if you have read the book *Soccer Training*, it is advised that you reread this chapter in this book because the largest portion of a player's shots should be driven shots. Any action in soccer can be broken down into essential components. **The four high-level guidelines of a driven shot in soccer, listed in chronological order to ensure precision, accuracy, and power are:**

1. Start diagonal to the ball.
2. Plant a foot away from the ball.
3. On the foot you are striking the ball with, have your toe down and out with your knee facing the target so that you can use the bone of your foot.
4. Follow through, land on your shooting foot, bring your back leg forward, and point your hips where you want to score.

To further understand the rules, consider the following:

1. **Stand at a 45° angle "diagonal" to the ball.** You want to be three to four steps from the ball to have a running start because the faster you are moving towards the ball, you will naturally have more power on your shot once you make contact. Comparatively, standing still and trying to strike the ball will reduce the power on your shot. As you stand 45° (diagonal) to the ball, you want your shoulders facing the ball as you approach it. Being directly behind the ball when you approach it ensures:

-Your shot is going to be diagonal across the goal's frame, which would result in a missed shot.

-You will have to change the part of your foot that you strike the ball with to have an accurate shot, which makes it so that it will not be a driven shot. It ends up either being a shot with the inside of your foot (a pass shot) or a toe ball/toe blow/toe poke with the toes of your foot.

2. **Run at the ball and plant (with the non-striking leg) one foot away from the ball.** The taller you are, the further you plant away. The smaller you are, the closer you plant to the ball, but for the average person, you will be planting about a foot away. Planting too close to the ball will make it so that you have to change the part of the foot that you are using to strike the ball. Therefore, it will no longer be a driven shot. Plant too far away from the ball and you will barely be able to reach the ball and will lose nearly all of the power on your shot. Make sure your plant foot is pointing at the portion of the net that you are looking to place the ball with your shot.

3. Fully contract your leg back to bring your foot behind your body. **Bending at the knee and the hip allows you to bring your foot back correctly.** If you only bend at the knee or the hip, you will lose a lot of muscle on the shot and therefore a lot of power. Bending at the knee allows your quadriceps to be engaged when striking the ball. Bending at the hip allows your hip flexor to be involved in the shot. Use them together and you will have a much harder shot. As you begin to drive your leg through the ball for a shot forcibly, make sure that your toe is down and out, and your knee is facing the target. Keep in mind that the target is not the net.

The target is where the goalie is not in the net. **Therefore, do not only point your knee at the net, but look to determine the portion of the net you want the ball to go towards.** Turning your knee so that it is facing out instead of towards the target will make it so that you are shooting the ball with the inside of your foot. For many soccer players, this tends to be more accurate because it is very close to the form of passing. However, because the inside of your foot is softer than the hardest portion of your foot that you use when you strike the ball with your toe down and out, it makes it so that you lose a lot of power on your shot.

If you practice exclusively with your toe facing down and out, taking inside of the foot shots will not be as comfortable. Being most comfortable with driven shots is for the best because the inside of the foot shots are not nearly as powerful and much easier to defend by a goalkeeper versus a driven shot if they are both placed in the same spot on the net. As your leg follows through the ball, use the bone of your foot (the hardest portion of your foot where the laces meet the leather towards the inside of your foot) to strike the ball. If you are looking for more power on your shot, striking the ball with the hardest portion of your foot will ensure there is power.

Think of the bone of your foot almost as if it is a baseball "bat," whereas further along your foot (towards your toes) is more like a "broom." **A "bat" is harder than a "broom," so using the "bat" to hit the ball will give you more power than using the "broom."** However, there is a time to use both portions of the top of your foot. If you are trying to loft the ball over a wall or a defender, striking the ball with the bone/"bat" of your foot will likely send it flying over the net or over the person which you are trying to loft the ball too. Striking the ball towards the top of your toes (the "broom") will allow the ball to go over the wall or defender, but then dip down because it will not have as much power.

4. After striking the ball, follow through with your leg to generate more power and accuracy on your shot. Follow through with the opposite leg as well. **Therefore, after you strike the ball, you will be landing past the spot on the field from which you struck the ball initially.** Essentially, strike the ball and follow through to a spot past where the ball was before you kicked the ball. Following through is similar if you were to "accidentally" throw a punch. You would not throw the punch with just your arm. You would use your entire body, including your hips, to turn at the waist to extend your arm as you throw the punch to have more power. You generate your power for nearly all athletic moves through your hips.

Similarly, you do not want to strike the ball with just your leg. You want to strike it using your leg as well as your entire body. The bone/bat of your foot is the portion that makes contact with the ball. Then, you will follow through your shot, land past the ball, and bring your planting leg forward while pointing your hips at your target. Again, the target is the portion of the net where the goalie is not located. Bringing your back leg/planting leg forward is key to easily allow you to turn your hips towards the portion of the net you want the ball to travel. **Additionally, visualizing your shot (or anything you are going to do in soccer or in life) before you take it is 70-80% as effective as actually having taken a practice shot from that same spot.**

Lastly, keeping your head down while you strike the ball keeps your chest over the ball. This keeps your form together for a more accurate shot and reduces the chance that the ball will go flying over the net. I know it is tough to keep your head down. I too like to watch all my shots go in, but **lifting your head will worsen your form**. Would you rather view all of your goals and have less of them or be the top scorer on the team, but only see a few of your goals?

Chapter 3

Ball Placement for Shots

When shooting you want to make sure your shots give you the highest probability that your team scores a goal. Notice it states "your team" and not "you" because as a good soccer player, your first ambition is to help the team win and then your second one is to grow individually as a soccer player. **During a game, if you dribble the ball or receive a pass and possess the ball between the goal and the penalty spot, you have to consider the goalie's positioning.** If he or she is coming out of the net and forcing you to shoot, you are going to want to shoot high and often towards the far post.

A shot higher on the frame of the net is necessary because a good goalie is going to cut off your ability to take a shot low and close to the ground. **Stopping shots low and close to the ground is how a goalie is trained when approaching you to cut off your angles for putting the ball into the back of the net.** However, if the goalie is not coming out of his net, then a shot driven close to the ground is more effective and will increase your probability of the ball going in the net. Even if the goalie saves the ball, their quick reaction time that stopped your objective of scoring the ball in their net is unlikely to catch or pick up the ball. Therefore, there will likely be a rebound that you or a teammate can shoot into the net. Also, low and driven shots tend to be much more accurate for nearly all soccer players.

From the penalty spot to the edge of the 18-yard box, this is still a good position for a low and driven shot to the far post. Low and driven to the far post means that you strike a shot that is ideally a foot off the ground and aimed a foot or two to the inside of the post farthest from you when you strike the ball. Low shots are more accurate and are very difficult for the keeper to save. Think about it, if a goalkeeper has to go from a standing position to a fully stretched out dive for the ball, this takes time. If the ball is shot several feet in the air towards the goal, generally the goalie is already standing and only has to jump a bit to punch the ball out of the way or to catch the ball. If he or she can easily catch the ball, he or she can quickly run to the edge of the 18-yard box with the ball and start his or her team's counterattack quickly.

Next, a shot that is directly on the ground is easier to save by a goalie than a shot slightly off of the ground. This is a reality because when a goalie extends a hand out to save a shot when they dive for the ball, they are trained to have their hand 3-4 inches off of the ground to ensure that any shot that is on the ground will be stopped. If you can shoot the ball a foot or two in the air, this makes it very easy for the goalie to miss the ball entirely or to only make contact with a piece of the ball. You will find that even if they can make contact with the ball, a well-driven shot will hit off their hand and still end up in the back of the net.

I am just like you in that I prefer all my goals to be perfectly upper 90, just like I see on SportsCenter's Top 10. However, you score so few of those shots in your career that you risk a lot of missed shots before you actually make one. Look at Lionel Messi for example, most of his goals are waist level or lower because he has learned that these shots increase your chances of scoring goals. **He is concerned about scoring more goals than scoring fancy goals.** Ask yourself this, would you rather be the player that scores 25 goals in a season and only one or two were perfect upper 90 shots or would you rather be the soccer player who scored ten goals in a season and eight or more of the goals where highlight reel worthy? Personally, I would much rather have a lot more goals than a few fancy goals because a goal is a goal, no matter how it went in. There are no bonus points for style on a shot from 35 yards away that dips and dives on its way to the back of the net.

When shooting from outside the 18-yard box, if you have a cannon of a shot, you can get away with a low and driven shot. However, the shot will likely have to be hard and driven higher in the air to ensure that the shot goes in. Shots in the air travel faster than shots on the ground because the grass or turf creates more friction on the traveling ball than the air would. Keep in mind that when you shoot from outside the 18-yard box, the goalie is normally a few feet out of the net, so there is a more likely to be some space to hit the ball over the keeper. **Be sure to consider that shooting high on the net increases the chance that you will miss the net.** When you aim for an upper 90 goal, if your shot is a foot too high, diagonal, or wide, the ball is going to hit the frame of the net or is going to miss the net altogether.

Understand that all of these ideal ball placements for shots are relative to where the

defender is in relation to your position on the soccer field. If they are one foot from you and sticking one of their legs out to potentially stop your shot, then you will have to shoot a little bit higher to make the ball go over their foot. Whereas, if you have a few yards between you and the defender, then it is easier for you to strike the ball low and close to the ground without being too concerned that they block the ball from going towards the net.

Chapter 4

Shooting with Your Opposite Foot

The form for shooting with your opposite foot is the exact same form as shooting with your dominant foot. Notice that in the title and the first sentence of this chapter, it says to shoot with your "opposite foot" and not your "weak foot." **By referring to your opposite foot as your weak foot, you are displaying a limiting belief.** Due to the fact that you are calling it your weak foot, you are going to treat it like a weak foot, which likely means you will not take the necessary steps to develop your opposite foot. You will likely avoid practicing with it and avoid developing it to the point to where you are comfortable using it in the game. How you perceive things in soccer and in life generally dictates how you will execute and become better. Most people agree that your beliefs help to shape the words you use, but few people realize the opposite is true too. The words you use help shape your beliefs, which is why you often hear from others that you should "watch what you say" because if you are not careful, you might end up believing something that holds you back.

Understand that you have to take a free kick just as good with either foot or that you should be able to shoot from 30 yards out just as easily and accurately with your opposite foot. Being able to shoot with your opposite foot means that if you are inside the 18-yard box, you should be comfortable going to the right foot or to the left foot, whichever foot is going make it easier for you to take a shot. A good defender is going to try to push you to your opposite foot. The opposing defender will give you a bit more space to push the ball, accelerate, and shoot with your opposite foot if you are willing to use it.

Any time that I am playing defense and I am going up against an attacker that only uses one of his feet to shoot the ball, I am very pleased. They are incredibly easy to shut down and it takes less effort to prevent them from shooting because you know which direction they are going to try to go. **All you have to do is give them space towards their opposite foot.** You know they are unlikely to utilize it and even if they do use it, they are not going to be comfortable enough with their opposite foot to take an effective shot. Yes, there are a few players that have made careers out of only using one foot, but those players are very few and far between, such as Mesut Ozil. Therefore, make it easy on yourself to succeed on the field by developing both feet.

Personally, I did not learn to use my opposite foot until I was 14 years old. As a child and early teenager, I had a lot of limiting beliefs. **One of those limiting beliefs was that "I was not naturally gifted at using my opposite foot, so this must mean I should not use it."** Keep in mind that it never registered with me that I was good with my dominant foot because I used it exclusively for the first 10 years of playing soccer. Finally, I swallowed my pride to realize that I needed to change. I needed to use the opposite foot but was so ashamed of my form that I was unwilling to use it in a practice or game. When I came to this conclusion, it was a summer that a World Cup was held, as they only occur every four years. I was inspired by the soccer players in those games and I was young enough that I had minimal responsibilities.

Therefore, every day over the course of that World Cup, I would watch the games and practice shooting for 30 minutes to an hour a day, 4 to 5 times a week with my opposite foot. I would go to the side of my parents' house and work on shooting with my opposite foot. I would either work on shooting for distance/power by striking the ball between my parents' house and my next door neighbor's house or take shots off of the wall of my parents' brick house to work on accuracy. (Note: ask your parents for permission before shooting soccer balls at your home).

Honestly, it started off very rough. I could not kick the ball with the bone of my foot more than 15-yards and my form was horrendous. It felt awkward and I can guarantee you that it looked awkward too. However, I made up my mind that I was going to keep practicing until I was able to use my opposite foot. **Notice what was said in the previous sentence. It stated, "I will keep doing it until."** I learned this mindset later in life from the mentor Jim Rohn, who reframed my view on how to approach a task, project, or situation that I wanted to attain a certain outcome. Luckily, I intuitively understood it at a young age. Your mindset is critical because generally, anytime you set out to do something, it will take longer and be more difficult than you originally planned. If your only process is to follow your plan and the plan does not work, then you give up. As a result, you still will not be able to use your opposite foot very well because you lacked the mindset and the consistency to keep practicing until you could do what you had initially set your mind to do.

Some tips when it comes to shooting with the bone of your opposite foot are:

1. **Make sure you are very angled to the ball** (45° at the absolute minimum, but ideally 60° to 75°) so that you can start becoming comfortable with pointing your toe down and out while using the bone of your opposite foot to strike the ball.

2. **Make sure to bend at the hip and the knee.** Too many of my trainees only bend at the hip which takes out your strongest muscle, your quadriceps, from being used to increase the power on your shot.

3. **Practice practice practice.** Make sure you do enough repetitions so that you start developing a consistent form. Obviously, you want this form to be perfect from the beginning, but if you dislike shooting with your opposite foot and have not really practiced using it, then your first goal is to become more comfortable using the opposite foot to strike the ball. Therefore, even if your form has room for improvement, work to have a more consistent form. If you work with someone to help correct your form and you lack any consistency on how you shoot with your opposite foot, it will be difficult for that person to try to help you fix your form. You will not have a few specific things to work on because every time you kick the ball, your form is considerably different.

Keep in mind that improving takes time. If you do not get it right away or even over the course of a few weeks, know that it took me about two and a half months to even become comfortable enough to use my opposite foot in practice. (Note: I was still uncomfortable even attempting an opposite footed shot in a game.) Therefore, if you feel uncomfortable using your opposite foot, practice using it in your free time outside of your house, on a soccer field, or on an open piece of land to work at developing an opposite foot that may be relied on to score.

A professional player that has a great story about using his opposite foot is David Villa. David Villa had played for Barcelona, Atlético Madrid, and the Spanish National Team, but was almost unable to because of an injury he sustained when he was four years old. Villa, who was a right-footed player suffered a broken right leg. With the guidance of his father to push him to use his left leg, he was able to come back stronger than other players his age because he started off so young being able to use both feet to dribble, pass, and shoot. His ability to use both feet laid the groundwork for a fantastic career as a striker in soccer.

Chapter 5

Correctly Practice Shooting in Warm-Ups

I cannot stress enough that you should always practice the way you are going to play. You definitely want to make sure you are practicing your shots the way you are likely going to shoot them in a game. You do not want to be a striker that is constantly practicing your defending skills or a goalie that is worried about how quick they can complete a 3-mile run because those things are not the best use of the majority of your practice time. They can help a bit, but it is not something that you should work on often in practice. They do not transfer all that well on to the soccer field for the position that you are playing.

Therefore, when you focus on shooting in practice or before a game, the ball should be rolling when you make contact with the ball! There is an excellent chance that nearly all of your shots will come after performing a skill, the ball is passed to you, or after you have pushed it out in front of you to take a shot. You will hardly ever have a shot where the ball is perfectly stopped. Let's be completely honest, if you can shoot with the ball rolling, you will have no problem being able to shoot with the ball stopped. Therefore, do not practice the thing that is easier and more comfortable to perform. Practice what is realistic in a game, which are shots when the ball is rolling.

I have a group of friends that I meet with to play soccer. They are a great group of guys, but I still wonder at this point, after having played with them for a handful of years, why they do not want to score more goals. When we warm up together, one other person besides myself actually performs a skill, pushes the ball, and then takes a shot. The rest of the team will only consider practicing with the ball when it is completely stopped. **On the one hand, I understand the fact that you may look silly during your first several attempts that you perform something you have never tried before.**

On the other hand, you will look a whole lot more silly if you cannot strike the ball while it is rolling, with your opposite foot, or with your first touch off a pass from a teammate. If you feel uncomfortable doing something you have never done before in front of others, then do not start doing it in front of others. Practice it on your own free time either on a field, in your backyard, or before anyone else gets to practice until you are comfortable using it when others can see. Therefore, it does not surprise me when my teammates do not take many shots and especially do not take many high-quality shots in a game because they do not practice the way they play.

Now, consider that if you are your team's free kick taker, then it is acceptable for you to work on your shots with the ball stopped. Even still, a person that takes free kicks is going to have many more shots over their career with the ball rolling than with the ball stopped. Therefore, they should only consider practicing free kicks with a small portion of their practice time. **Let's be honest, if you cannot score while the ball is rolling, your coaches probably are not even going to consider you as their player to take free kicks.** The fact that coaches do not normally select players to take free kicks that cannot score in regular game situations was something that I did not realize for the first ten or so years of my playing career. Honestly, it has only sunken in while writing this chapter. Not knowing this wisdom when I needed it is saddening because had I practiced with the ball rolling, I likely would have scored a lot more goals in my career and had the opportunity to take a lot more free kicks because the coach viewed me as a goal scorer. Because I did not score that many goals in the regular play of a game, early in my playing career, my coaches often did not look to me to take the free kicks.

For example, when I played high school varsity soccer, I had an extremely dangerous free kick because that is how I always practiced. I could place the ball upper 90 consistently. I had terrific form, I kept my head down, and I could easily shoot the ball over any wall the goalie made with players from his team. **The only problem was that no one cared because I could not score in a typical game situation, so why would they look for me to do it when the ball is stopped and the coach could select any player on the field to take the shot?** Why would the coach have someone take a free kick that cannot produce in a regular game situation?

Honestly, I do not blame the coach looking back on his decisions. I would have done the same thing if I was in his shoes. **Keep in mind that when the ball is rolling, you want to plant a foot to the side and a foot in front of the ball.** However, when you go to shoot the ball with the ball stopped, you plant one foot to the right or left of the ball, depending on which foot will be striking the ball. Do not plant in front of the ball because the ball is not rolling. Therefore, it is so important to practice the way you play. Not only for shooting but other topics too. Make sure the ball is rolling and you are going at least at 85% or 90% of the speed you would be using to strike the ball in a game when you are shooting in a warm-up or practice.

Chapter 6

Beating a Defender

To beat a defender when dribbling, make sure that you aggressively push the ball and explode away after doing a foot skill. The three essential reasons for this are:

1. **It provides space between you and the defender.** Therefore, you will have slightly more time to pick your head up to see where the goalie is and where to aim your shot.

2. If you accelerate after pushing the ball, you will have more speed running to the ball. **If you have more speed running to the ball, you are naturally going to have a more powerful shot.** For example, imagine you are standing still and you strike a shot with your foot planted next to the ball versus having a good three to four step run up on the ball. You will kick it a lot harder with a running start when your momentum, your body, and your hips can go through the ball when you strike your shot.

3. An aggressive push past the defender will allow you to be closer to the net. **The closer you are to the net, the more accurate you will be as the net becomes bigger.**

Additionally, being closer to the net, the goalie is going to have less time to react to stop your shot.

4. **When you explosively push the ball closer to the net, the goalkeeper will have less time to react to your shot.** If the goalie has less time to react to your shot, the greater the chance that your shot will go in. Now keep in mind that pushing the ball too far will give the ball to the opponent's goalkeeper.

Pushing the ball past a defender is best suited for when you have just performed a foot skill. You push the ball with the outside portion of your laces about 5-7 yards behind the defender. Please keep in mind faster players can afford to push the ball further than slower players. Also, a 5-7 yard push works great when you are going against only one defender, but if there is another defender behind the defender you are approaching, you would want to first use a foot skill. Then, you would use a smaller push of the ball that will only go 2-3 yards. This will help you avoid pushing the ball into the supporting defender's feet.

It is critical that you go into a game with the mindset that you are going to beat defenders that will allow you to take shots. If your current mindset has you a little bit scared to go against a defender 1v1, you are likely not going to be successful. You have to have confidence in yourself, so as you read this book and implement the tips, tricks, tweaks, and techniques this book mentions, you will gain confidence in your ability to beat a defender and strike a quality shot on net.

Consider the fact that a defender is typically running backward when you are going against them. **Therefore, it is crucial to understand that a defender running backward will not be as quick as an attacker running forward.** As a result, an attacker's speed is critical because the higher the pace the forward attacks with, the harder it will be for the defender to keep up while staying balanced. Additionally, when you explode past a defender, there is a brief moment when the defender is transitioning from running backward to turning their bodies to run forward to keep up with you. If your initial push is explosive enough, the defender will not have time to transition their body's momentum from running backward to running forward quickly enough to stop you. Watch Eden Hazard, the Chelsea and Belgium National team member to see a player that can effectively take first touches and push the ball efficiently past defenders, seemingly with ease.

Furthermore, you do not have to be entirely past the defender to take a shot. All you need is just a little bit of space to create a shot that is effective and on target. If the defender has been covering you well during the game, shooting into their shins/ankles is not going to help your team at all, but keep in mind that you miss 100% of the shots you do not take. It is much more important for a soccer team to try to increase the volume of its shots because more shots result in more chances for the ball to go in.

Let's play out a situation; a team that takes 30 shots in a game compared to a team that takes five really good shots. The team that takes 30 shots is still probably going to win because there are more opportunities for the goalie to accidentally make a mistake, for the shooting team to have a lucky shot, or for the goalie to give up a rebound resulting in a teammate putting the ball into the back of the net.

Chapter 7

Heading the Ball

Heading the ball is a skill to be mastered by all soccer players, but is especially vital to those trying to score and those trying to prevent the other team from scoring. Since this book is on shooting and finishing, this chapter will emphasize being able to head the ball into the back of the net or into an area that will allow the ball to be easily scored.

First, when doing a header in soccer, it is essential that you contract your body forward by pulling your arms backward. **Contracting your body, in addition to your**

neck, allows you to snap your body forward to quickly accelerate your head towards the ball, which will dramatically increase the power of your headers. Make sure to head through the ball to ensure even more power and most importantly, more accuracy. This portion is easily learned, but being able to judge the flight of the ball to time your jump takes practice and experience.

Having accurate and powerful headers is critical because even the most powerful header is still going to be much slower than a soccer player's shot. Therefore, the goalie will likely have more time to react to stop your attempt to score, which means your placement of the ball after heading it must be great. Most forwards do not include heading the ball as a part of their arsenal of ways to score because they often lack the power, accuracy, and/or jumping ability to have headers be a meaningful portion of their game. If you are a 5'5" forward, you are better off focusing more on your speed, your ability to shoot, and your ability to dribble than you would be on headers. The opposite holds true if you are a 6'5" forward. Being able to score with your head is a must and this is something that would be very important for you to practice.

When doing a header, use your forehead, not the top of your head. Too often I will see trainees using the top portion of their head, which generally just sends the ball flying over the net. It is tough to have any accuracy when the tops of their heads are used because your eyes are off the ball for a significant amount of time. Additionally, to ensure that there is accuracy on your headers, you must keep your eyes open until a split second before the ball hits your head. I say this from experience because I recall a high school game in which a beautiful cross was played to me with the ball soaring over everybody else's heads. I was at the far post while the goalie and the rest of the defenders were at the near post. Because I shut my eyes too early, I did not have an accurate header and missed a wide-open net against one of our local rivals. This mistake is forever etched in my memory. Though we often learn more from our mistakes than from our successes, it is funny how the errors tend to be remembered much longer than all of the great plays you performed.

On corner kicks, as a forward or midfielder, do not just head the ball because it is close to you when it is crossed in the air. If you are only able to make contact with the ball using the top of your head, your header definitely will not go in. In this instance you should miss the header entirely and hope a teammate is behind you with a better chance to head the ball. Make sure this concept is communicated to teammates because frequently teammates will not even go up for a header if it looks like you were going to go and head it yourself. **Therefore, make sure they know you will be making a snap judgment in the air whether you will take the header or not.** Also, make sure to tell your other forwards and midfielders that if they are behind you, they should still go up for the ball as if you were not going to head it at all. Tell them there is a decent chance you are just going to let the ball go by because it is going to be a low probability header for you anyways.

Being able to use good judgment in soccer is what differentiates the good forwards from the great forwards. Great forwards are not only concerned with their own success and how many times they can get on the stat sheet, but they are also concerned with how often their team can win. A great player knows deep down that their team having success will bring them more recognition in the long run anyways. If a cross or corner kick is played towards the top of the 18-yard box, then recognize that unless you are already at the professional level in soccer, there is a very low probability that you will be able to have enough power on your header to get the ball past a keeper that has 18 yards worth of time to react. Therefore, be reasonable with your headers. If you are at the penalty spot or closer to the opponent's net, this is an appropriate time to use a header to score. Otherwise, if you are further away than the penalty spot, it is highly recommend against using a header to try to score.

Furthermore, the form for heading the ball is just as important as being open enough to attempt the header. I consulted a fellow soccer player and defender, Toni Sinistaj, on what he hates most that attackers do to find space. **He pointed out that forwards that are constantly moving to evade the defender marking him or her are the hardest to cover. He also mentioned that he especially dislikes when a forward recruits other teammates to set picks, so they can obstruct his path to shut that striker down who is looking to be on the end of a header.** Therefore, work to become as sneaky and evasive as possible. Also, aim to travel in the defender's blind spot. A defender's blind spot is where they have to choose between viewing the ball or seeing you. Defenders hate this because it makes it much easier for a forward to create space to receive a pass.

In conclusion, be sure to use your upper body to contract your head faster than you could if you just contracted your head at the neck. Too many soccer players, myself included at times, will allow the ball to hit them in the head and then based on where their head is positioned, the ball will deflect towards the net or be a pass to a teammate. **Not extending at the neck creates**

very weak headers that can be easily fixed by using the entire body to have a much more powerful header, which increases the chance that the ball will sneak past the goalkeeper. Additionally, use your forehead and not the top of your head, as it will hurt a little bit less and will be more accurate.

Next, do not just head the ball to head the ball. **Make sure if you are going to attempt to head the ball, then your header must have a chance of going in.** If your header does not have a chance to score, then just let the ball go by for another teammate to get a head or foot on the ball. Lastly, because there is limited power on headers, do not use a header unless you are at the penalty spot or closer to the net in a game. If you do attempt to head the ball at the 18-yard box, understand that it is likely going to be an easy grab for the goalie whom will quickly pass the ball out of his box and start a counterattack against your team.

Chapter 8

Pass Shot

A pass shot, also known as a finesse shot, is similar to a driven shot in that there is no spin on the ball. However, it differs in that it is often more accurate, but is not nearly as powerful. **The four guidelines of a pass shot are:**

1. Start behind the ball.
2. Plant next to the ball.
3. On the foot you are striking the ball with, have your toe up and out, your heal down, and your knee pointing sideward so you can use the inside of your foot.
4. Follow through, land on your shooting foot, bring your back leg forward, and point your hips where you want the ball to go.

To further understand the rules, consider the following:

1. **Start three to four steps behind the ball to have a running start.** The faster you are moving towards the ball, the more power you will naturally have on your shot. A few step run-up is helpful for a pass shot because you are not striking the ball with the hardest part of your foot. Comparatively, standing still and trying to hit the ball will reduce the power on your shot. You want your shoulders facing the ball as you approach it. Being directly behind the ball when you approach it ensures your shot is going to be straight where you are pointing your hips.

2. Run at the ball and plant (with the non-striking leg) next to the ball. **Planting close to the ball will make it so that you turn your foot and strike the ball with the inside of your foot.** Plant too far away from the ball and you will barely be able to reach the ball and will lose nearly all of the power on your shot. Make sure your plant foot is pointing at the portion of the net where you are looking to place the ball.

3. **Contract your leg back at the hip to bring your foot behind your body with only a slight bend in the knee.** As you begin to forcibly drive your leg through the ball for a shot, make sure that your toe is up and out and your

knee is pointing sideward so you can use the inside of your foot.

This form is identical to that of a pass, but you are adding a full body follow through to have a much stronger pass. The inside of your foot is softer than the hardest portion of your foot that you use when striking the ball for a driven shot. As a result, a pass shot has less power versus a driven shot, but because the form is similar to that of a pass, you will likely be more much more accurate.

4. After striking the ball, follow through with your leg to generate more power and accuracy on your shot. Follow through with the opposite leg as well. **Therefore, after you strike the ball, you will be landing past the spot on the field from which you struck the ball initially.** Essentially, strike the ball and follow through to a spot past where the ball was before you kicked it.

Pass shots are best used when shooting at the net from close range. Ideally, if you are between the penalty spot and the 18-yard box or closer to the net, then the pass shot is appropriate since shooting accuracy is a top priority when you are close to the net. Power matters too and that is why you should follow through with your leg as well as your entire body to hit a harder shot, but a well-placed shot is going to have a higher chance of scoring when you are to the net and the goalkeeper has so little time to react.

An example of a player known for taking pass shots is David Luiz. David Luiz has played at the club level for teams such as PSG and Chelsea. He has performed at the international level for the powerhouse Brazil. David Luiz's goal against Columbia in the 2014 World Cup is an excellent example of a pass shot. He used a pass shot from farther out than is recommend for most players, but when you can have the ball zigzag as much as he did, then it will likely be effective given the goalie will have a tough time tracking the ball to make the save.

Chapter 9

2v1s

When there is a 2v1, where you and another attacker are going against only one defender (and the goalie) to score, the first thing that should be a natural reaction is that you have to be as quick as possible. You have a huge advantage given that you have twice as many people attacking as the other team has defending. Therefore, it is essential that you use your explosiveness and your teammate's speed to keep this advantage alive without allowing defensive support to come and catch up with you and your teammate. **Keeping your advantage means taking large attacking touches to cover as much space in as little amount of time as possible while being reasonable given where the defender is in relation to you.** Obviously, you do not want to take too big of a touch that goes right into the defender's feet or out of bounds, but often players take a bunch of small touches that require too much time to cover the space you have available. Not to forget, I often see the person with the ball using skills that take too long when a jab or scissor would have been perfect.

In a 2v1, this is one of the best times to read the defender's body and what he or she makes available

for you. Specifically, if the defender is shutting you down and leaving your teammate open, then play a ball a few yards in front of your teammate so that he or she does not have to break his or her stride to receive the ball. A ball played a few yards in front of a teammate during a 2v1 will increase the chances that your teammate will be able to take a shot on net. (Note: For a forward, have it in your mind that a goal is as good as an assist. Either one means that there is a goal added to your team's score.)

If the defender is cutting off the passing lane, then even better! You can simply shoot the ball on target because you have space to do so. **In this situation, do not worry about your teammate thinking that you are selfish if you do not pass the ball. If the defender is giving you an open shot close to the net, then take it!** You will not have to worry about completing a pass to a teammate who will then hopefully receive it well and shoot the ball. Remember, when a defender is cutting down your passing lane towards a teammate, shoot the ball!

A mindset that I had for many years and even still have to a small degree today is that if there is a 2v1 situation and I do not pass the ball, then I am a selfish player that is only looking out for my own interests and do not care about anyone else on the team. However, this is the furthest thing from the truth as long as you can read and understand what the defender is allowing you to do. In fact, it is more detrimental to your team if you make a pass while the defender is cutting off the passing lane than it is for you to shoot. **Sure, maybe you will feel a little bad and think that you should have passed in that situation so the other person could have received the glory but remember that your most significant objective in this situation is to help your team achieve its purpose of winning the game.** If you have an open shot and a clogged passing lane, then you better shoot the ball. Do not worry about feeling bad because by taking the shot in that instant, you are doing what is best for the team.

Now, the reverse holds true too if you are the person without the ball in the 2v1. **Do not expect the pass if the defender is giving your teammate a shot and definitely do not give your teammate a hard time for being selfish if they did the correct thing.** However, we are probably similar in that we would rather score than earn an assist or not be on the stat sheet at all. Therefore, make sure you are making a quality run into space. A quality run is essential because if the defender decides to no longer cut off the passing lane but to defend your teammate with the ball, this will allow the passing lane to be open. As a result, make sure that you are in an appropriate position to receive a pass or to run on to receive a pass that will significantly increase your team's chances of scoring.

Furthermore, make sure that you are staying far enough away from your teammates to provide space for a pass that the defender cannot catch up to and will allow you enough time to take a quality shot on net. **Each 2v1 will be slightly different from the next, but in every game-situation, one of the most important things to consider is that you have to be onside when the pass is made!** Messing up the 2v1 because you were slightly offside is a sure-fire way to make it so your teammate will be even more hesitant to pass you the ball in the game going forward. Additionally, it is an easy way to take the momentum away from your team's advancement on the field and in their spirits/inner dialogue. Ruining a 2v1 reduces your team's energy because you blew a high probability situation because you were not aware of your location in relation to the defender that is defending you and your teammate. Therefore, when you are the teammate without the ball, it is a good rule of thumb to be lined up with the ball to make sure that you will not be offside if your teammate plays a pass to you.

In conclusion, for a situation that involves two attackers versus one defender, make sure that you are explosive by taking large touches and read the defender to see if they are attempting to defend you or cut off the passing lane. If they are defending you, then pass. If they are cutting off the passing lane, then shoot. Do not worry about appearing selfish because you are performing the action that will help your team succeed.

Chapter 10

Shooting with the Outside of your Foot

For this chapter, Ricardo Quaresma was studied, as he has had many spectacular goals with the outside of his foot for his club and country. Additionally, Chris Wolowski, a fellow player and friend was consulted as he has made quite the career out of being able to strike the ball however necessary to shoot the ball on target, while avoiding his shot being blocked by defenders. Frequently, this means he uses an outside of the foot shot, also known as a Trivela, to increase his chances of scoring. **An outside of the foot shot is extremely effective for the following reasons:**

1. Deceptive to the defender and goalkeeper on when you will shoot the ball.
2. A significant amount of curve to shoot around a defender or goalkeeper, as well as to pass around the other team.
3. Excellent for helping keep your knee over the ball on volleys that you shoot on net.

An outside of the foot shot is one of the most deceptive shots in the game. You strike the ball with the same portion of your foot that you would use if you were to dribble the ball. Therefore, it does not look like you will shoot the ball most times when you go to actually strike it. Having a shot that does not look like a shot is terrific because most soccer players that strike the ball with a pass shot or driven shot will find that defenders are often able to jump in front of the shot to block it with their legs and body. Since defenders often slide or lunge to be in front of the ball when you are shooting, shot fakes are often very useful. More often than not though, you will be shooting and not doing a shot fake, which may result in the defender making contact with a piece of the ball to reduce the power and accuracy on your shot. Often, this leads to a failed attempt to place the ball in the net.

In fact, in a recent game I played in, there were two occasions that I went up against the same defender and did a shot fake with my right foot and then proceeded to push the ball to my left and shoot it with my left foot. On both attempts, the defender stepped in front of my shot fake as well as lunged out far enough to be in front of the actual shot. In all honesty, I was pretty blown away that he was able to do that because my shot fakes are usually very believable and defenders tend to dive in and do not have time to recover after they have committed to blocking what ended up being a shot fake. **However, had I been shooting with the outside of my foot, there would have been a better chance that the defender**

would have never dove in front of my shot. He would have likely assumed that I was taking another dribble, as opposed to shooting the ball. Being able to strike an unblocked shot is significant because both of the opportunities were great chances for me to score.

Next, an outside of the foot shot is handy because it allows you to have a curve in the path that the ball takes. The curve is similar to that of a bent shot but often with more power similar to a driven shot. A bending shot is tremendous because you can take more shots that are not going to be blocked because the defender assumes you are still dribbling instead of shooting and you will have more power on those shots than you would with a pass shot or a bent shot.

The outside of the foot shot allows you to diversify the way you can shoot the ball on target to continually keep the defenders and goalie guessing. **Per the image, use the portion of your foot where the leather of the outside of your show meets the laces.** When a defender knows you can use any part of your foot or can use either one of your feet, they tend to give you more space. When they give you more space, it makes it even easier for you to have time to shoot, pass, dribble, or do whatever you need to do on the field. The defender will give you a certain amount of space and respect because they do not want to be beat, so they are hoping that you will pass the ball off to someone else and they will have considered their job done because they did not allow such a good soccer player to continue with the ball. Also, because your outside of the foot shot or pass is going to be a bit curved, this enables you to pass or shoot around the goalkeeper by bending it in or to find a passing lane that would not have been there otherwise if you were not able to curve the ball when you passed it.

Outside of the foot shots are very dangerous when you are inside of the 18-yard box. They are similarly threatening when you are attacking down the sideline and cross the ball into the box before the defender even realizes what you are doing. **Being able to bend the ball, but still have a significant amount of power on your**

shot because you are using your laces when you are shooting with the outside of your foot is extremely effective. Outside of the foot shots are great to add to your arsenal of ways to shoot.

Keep in mind that you should only develop the outside of the foot shot once you have become very comfortable with a driven shot and an inside of the foot shot. **Please note that shooting with the outside of your foot involves you turning your toes down and in to hit the ball with the laces of your cleats, which is directly on top of the bone of your foot.** Performed this way, it allows you to use the hardest part of your foot to have more power on your shot.

Lastly, shooting a volley with the outside of your foot will often allow you to keep your knee over the ball even more so than striking the ball with the driven shot form while the ball is outside of your shoulder. **When striking the ball out of the air with the outside of the foot form, your natural tendency will be to have your shoulders over the ball and striking the ball underneath you.** Whereas when you strike the ball using the driven shot form, it is very easy for you to make contact slightly too low on the ball that forces you to blast the ball way over the net.

Additionally, striking with the driven form makes it easy for you to tilt your shoulders back and send the ball sailing over the net. Yes, for an outside of the foot shot you can definitely position your foot under the ball when you strike your shot while having your shoulders back. It will guarantee that the shot soars over the net, but the outside of the foot shot increases the chance that this will not happen versus a standard driven shot. **As a soccer player, it is all about improving the probability that your shot will go in.** For example, shots taken close to the net are more likely to go in than shots from further away. Harder shots are more likely to go in than softer shots. Well-aimed shots are more likely to go in than poorly aimed shots. Combine these together for a powerful, accurate, and close-range shot that I guarantee will result in more goals than you ever dreamed possible.

In conclusion, shooting with the outside of your foot allows you to be deceptive to defenders and the goalkeeper. It allows you to bend the ball when you shoot and it decreases the likelihood that volleys will be shot over the net. Master the driven shot and the pass shot before you spend a considerable amount of time on the outside of the foot shot. It is an intermediate to an advanced level style of shooting. **One common trap that players often fall into when it comes to shooting with the outside of their foot is that they master shooting**

with only their dominant foot and do not develop their opposite foot. The soccer player can compensate by just shooting with the outside of their dominant foot instead of developing their opposite foot. You probably will not make it as far as you want in your soccer career if you cannot use both of your feet. The number of opportunities in a game that exists for you to use your opposite foot are tremendous and for you to go your entire career without using both feet is very detrimental for your confidence too.

Chapter 11

One-Time Shooting vs. Taking a First Touch Then Shooting

When it comes to deciding whether to use a first touch to shoot or a first touch to settle the ball and then the second touch to shoot on net, the two significant things to consider are the amount of time you have and your distance to the goal. **As the distance increases between you and the goal, you want to consider taking an additional touch.** It is harder to aim a shot off of a cross or a pass when you strike it with your first touch than it is to take a touch to help settle the ball and then to shoot the ball.

Similarly, the more time that you have means more space for you to take a touch to settle the ball. An extra touch makes it easier to know exactly where that ball is going to be located to increase the accuracy of your shots. **Additional things to keep in mind are the type of soccer player you are.** If you are someone that is good at shooting and can finish consistently off of a cross or a pass, then consider taking a first touch shot even if you are not that close to the net. If you are outside of the 18-yard box, you probably want to take a first touch that controls the ball and then your second touch would be your shot on net.

For example, if you are between the penalty spot and the net, you will want your first touch to be a shot. First, it will likely catch the goalie off guard. Even a shot that is a bit inaccurate is still going to have a very high chance of going in because you are so close to the net and the goalie has little time to react. Also, because you are inside of the penalty spot of the other team's 18-yard box, you better believe that you are going to have defenders working their butts off to shut you down. As a result, you will not likely have time to take an additional touch before shooting.

Chapter 12

Bent Shot

In this chapter, you will notice that the form for a bent shot is similar to a driven shot, but includes a few fundamental differences. **The four guidelines of a bent/curved shot, listed in order, to ensure precision, accuracy, and power are:**

1. Start diagonal to the ball.
2. Plant next to the ball. (Do not plant a foot away as you would for a driven shot).
3. On the foot you are striking the ball with, use the bone of your foot, keep your toe down and out with your knee pointed OUT, similar to a pass.
4. Strike the ball so that it is spinning when it comes off of your foot. Follow through, but be sure to CROSS your feet and then bring the plant foot around to uncross your feet, while you point your hips where you want the ball to go.

To further understand the rules, consider the following:

1. **For a bent shot, you want to stand at a 45° angle similar to that of a driven shot or you can stand directly behind the ball.** You want to be three or four steps from the ball to have a running start to the ball because the faster you are moving towards the ball, you will naturally have more power on your shot once you make contact. A running start is essential for a bent shot because often, you will not use the bone of your foot when striking the ball as you would with a driven shot, so you will have a less powerful shot when bending the ball. The few step run-up allows you to have more power on the shot than you would have if you kicked the ball from a dead stop. As you stand 45° (diagonal) to the ball, you

want your shoulders facing the ball as you approach the ball.

2. **Run at the ball and plant (with the non-striking leg) next to the ball.** If you plant too far away from the ball, you will barely be able to reach the ball and will lose nearly all of the power on your shot. Make sure your plant foot is pointing at the portion of the net that you are looking to place the ball with your shot.

3. **Fully contract your leg back to bring your foot behind your body when shooting a bent shot using the bone of your foot.** Bending at the knee and the hip allows you to bring your foot back correctly to increase the power on your shot. **If you are shooting a bent shot with the inside of your foot, then there is only a slight bend at the knee and full contraction at the hip.** For many soccer players, this tends to be more accurate because it is very close to the form of passing. Not fully extending at the knee coupled with not directly using the bone of the foot is the reason bent shots with the inside of your foot are not as powerful as bent shots with the bone of your foot, but often because more of your foot makes contact with the ball when using the inside of your foot, you are better able to make the ball curve when you shoot. Bending at the knee allows your quadriceps to be engaged when striking the ball. Bending at the hip allows

your hip flexor to be involved in the shot. Combine them together and you will have a much harder shot. As you begin to drive your leg forcibly through the ball for a shot, make sure that your toe is down and out for a driven bent shot. Make sure your toe is up and your heel is down for an inside of the foot bent shot.

4. **After striking the ball, follow through with your leg across your body, so that you end up crossing your legs. Follow through with the opposite leg as well, so that your legs will become uncrossed after the shooting leg crossed them.** Therefore, after you strike the ball, you will be landing next to the spot on the field from which you struck the ball initially. You would land past where you struck the ball on a driven shot. Finish off the shot by pointing your hips at the portion of the net where the goalie is not located.

In summary, a bent shot:
-Requires the plant foot to be next to the ball and not a foot away as with a driven shot.
-Performed with the bone of your foot, but your knee is pointing out (instead of towards the target when shooting a driven shot).
-Demands that you cross your legs after the shot to have the ball to curve/bend.

If you are taking a right-footed bent shot, you should generally be taking a shot towards the right side of the net. **Focusing on which way your shot bends and which portion of the net you are striking at is significant.** The ball will curve away from the net and then come back just inside the post when you bend the ball with the inside of your right foot towards the right post of the net. The ball curving away from the net and bending back just before the ball reaches the net is how you can curve the ball around the goalie. If you did a right-footed bent shot towards the left post, the ball would bend in front of the keeper, making it easier for them to save it. The opposite is true for a left-footed bent shot attempt.

An example of a legendary player with a very tactical bent shot is David Beckham. In fact, David Beckham has a soccer saying inspired by his shooting form: "bend it like Beckham." This saying originated because of how much curve he was able to have on his bent crosses and shots. Watch David Beckham on YouTube for outstanding examples of the way curved shots and crosses can be very deceptive to the goalie and extremely dangerous for the opponent's defense.

Chapter 13

When to Shoot vs. When to Pass

Knowing when to shoot and when to pass is the difference between being a teammate and a selfish individual soccer player. For this chapter, unless it is specified otherwise, let us assume that we are within 20 yards from the net.

First and foremost, if you are not at the very least within 25 yards of the net, you probably do not want to shoot. Shooting from further than 25 yards away is only acceptable when the goalie is well out of their net or there are just a few seconds left on the clock and the only option is to launch the ball while hoping for the best. You generally do not want to pass to a teammate when he or she is being covered by two or more people unless they are known for being physical and able to possess a ball in pressure. This type of pass often risks the other team stealing the ball and if it is on your half of the field, it can quickly turn into a goal for the other team.

Next, you generally want to take a shot when you have it. **Passes are appropriate when you create a much easier shot for a teammate.** You should shoot and not pass when the person you are passing to would have just as difficult of a shot as you do. If the teammate you are considering passing the ball to does not have a much higher chance of finishing their shot, then you increase the chance the other team will obtain the ball. Why is this? Because instead of you shooting, you now have to complete an accurate pass to your teammate, they have to take an accurate first touch (assuming they are not shooting a one-time shot), and then they must strike an accurate shot. All these additional steps increase the chance of a mistake being made. Now keep in mind, your ability to make an accurate pass increases with experience as a soccer player, so it becomes easier to rely on your ability to connect a series of passes. However, also relying on their first touch and their ability to finish should be weighed against your ability to shoot and score. If they are much better at finishing, then pass, but if they are only marginally better, then consider taking the shot yourself.

Remember that an okay shot is better than a stolen pass or a bad first touch that results in no shot. Increase the number of goals you score by increasing the number of shots you take. Also, make sure your teammates are aware of your general intention to shoot, so they will know to hustle to place all the rebounds into the back of the net.

Now, understand that soccer is a team sport, so in most instances, passes will be very beneficial because the ball can travel a lot faster than a soccer player. Use this to your advantage to move the ball past several players at once. Passing the ball past several opponents is something that individually dribbling each defender cannot do. Additionally, passing will help exhaust the other team because they will constantly be working to shut down passing lanes. However, make sure you are confident in your abilities to both pass and dribble to give you options on defeating the other team.

There is a certain amount of experience that is needed to know exactly when to pass or shoot. **Trust in your ability to perform as a soccer player and take shots in games to practice the repetitions that will make you better later in your soccer career.** However, if the pass makes more sense to score, then be a team player and earn the assist! After all, the soccer player that goes out to help the team win and is also striving to learn and grow in the process will be much better off than the soccer player that does not have any specific intentions when playing in a game.

Chapter 14

1v2s

When taking on two defenders, it is critical that you, as the striker, are looking to make it as easy as possible for you to score. Therefore, ask yourself if taking on two defenders will be easier or will it be easier only to attack against one?

A good defender is going to force you into their supporting teammate, but a good striker is going to travel to the outside slightly where they only have to beat one defender to shoot the ball. To do this, all it takes is a simple foot skill, such as a jab/feint or scissors in the direction towards the second defender and then push the ball to the outside of the first defender you are attacking against to find space away from both defenders to shoot. Also, this is good advice for a 1v3 where you are attacking three defenders. The overarching goal is to have a more favorable advantage that a 1v1 provides over a 2v1. Aim only to take on one defender to find the space for you to take a shot if you have no one on your team supporting you. Conversely, pick your head up to see if you have any support that may make your situation a little bit more favorable.

Your ability to use foot skills versus your ability to shoot will determine how close you should aim to be to the net in the 1v2 before shooting. If you are a good shooter, then definitely only try to beat the first defender to find the space to shoot. However, if you see yourself much better with your foot skills, then consider taking on the second. However, a good attacker will only beat a defender one time in a run. Changing speed and exploding after a skill ensures you do not have to waste time and energy to travel past a defender you have already beat. Furthermore, attempting to beat a defender twice increases your chances of failure. Therefore, make sure to be explosive after any dribbling and accelerate away from each defender as you beat them with your foot skills.

Chapter 15

Striking the Ball Out of the Air

When striking the ball out of the air, there are four key things to consider to increase your probability of success on every shot. **Implement these four things into your training and the number of shots you convert to goals out of the air will increase dramatically:**

1. Head down.
2. Perfect practice makes perfect.
3. Know where you are aiming.
4. Inside of the foot increases accuracy
and the bone of the foot increases power.

First, you absolutely must keep your head down anytime you are shooting the ball out of the air or anytime you make contact with the ball period. **Keeping your head down keeps your form together and makes it much easier for you to concentrate on your follow through, striking the ball with the correct portion of your foot, and squaring your hips towards the target.** I have had countless trainees (and yes, even myself too at times) be so excited that they just shot the ball that they want to see it go in, so they look up. Looking up immediately after shooting turns the frame of the body and creates an inaccurate shot that often misses. Keeping your head down better ensures that all the different points of shooting come together on every shot.

Second, when it comes to soccer or any sport for that matter, "perfect practice makes perfect." This is a saying that one of my trainees taught me. I had heard many times before that "practice makes perfect," but if you are consistently practicing doing something the wrong way, you habituate it and ingrain it in your form and in your thoughts in a way that is not as productive as it should be. Therefore, it is essential to make sure that you practice with the correct form anytime you are doing something.

To understand the correct form, you can ask others that are where you want to be (other players who are phenomenal at shooting), you can read books like this, you can watch YouTube videos, you can hire a soccer trainer, and you can do all these things together to gain the knowledge to ensure you are starting with the right form.

Tiger Woods, a famous golfer, is one of the best examples of this concept. Even though there has been much controversy surrounding his personal life in prior years, it is well known that at the pinnacle of his career, he was the best golfer of his time. However, towards the beginning of his professional career, his coach informed him that his swing had room for major improvements. Keep in mind that Tiger Woods was a golfer that had spent well over a decade using a certain form on his golf swing. His coach revealed this to him after he had already won several pro tournaments. Tiger Woods realized his coach was right and chose to change his form after, by most people's accounts, he had "made it" as a professional golfer. Switching his form ended up being a very profitable decision for him because he went from being a really good golfer to an excellent golfer that was expected to win every tournament he entered. Therefore, the point of this story is to start out practicing with the correct form to avoid creating unproductive habits that are not beneficial for your soccer career. Gain the knowledge of the proper form to give yourself a competitive advantage when practicing and playing soccer. Understand that you must follow up the instruction with a high number of repetitions to make sure you are doing it correctly every time and the proper form because automatic for you.

Third, knowing what you plan to do before you receive the ball is huge in soccer. Always know exactly where you are looking to strike the ball, where you are going before you receive a pass, and where you are going to make a run to become open for a teammate or to create space for them to attack more efficiently. Too many of my trainees shoot just to shoot. They do not shoot with the intent to score by placing their shot in a location where the goalie is not. Although I do not want to admit it, I find myself doing this from time to time too. Knowing exactly where on the frame you want the ball to go is going to increase your accuracy tremendously. If I just tell the trainees that after they are done with a passing/foot skills sequence to shoot on net, in the shooting and finishing classes that I conduct, the shots end up all over the place. Many of the shots are over the net and there is very little consistency and accuracy for most players.

However, when I place a cone or a stake in the ground and tell them exactly where I want them to shoot the ball, their accuracy increases 10X. Even if they miss the target, their shots are much closer to where they wanted them to go than when I only said to shoot on net. Having a tiny target that you are aiming for makes it a lot easier to score because even if you miss a small target, there is a good chance the ball is going to go in. **Remember, "aim small to miss small."** If you are shooting at the entire net when you go to strike the ball, you are shooting at a big target. It is easy for the ball to go wide or over the net. Furthermore, if not over or wide, the shot will likely be at the goalie, which will make it very easy for the goalkeeper to stop. Therefore, any time you go to strike the ball out of the air, make sure that you have a portion of the net in mind where you want the ball to go. Do not just shoot to shoot.

Fourth, the distance you are from the net determines which portion of your foot you strike the ball with out of the air. If you are towards the edge of the 18-yard box or further out than the 18-yard box, you should use the bone of your foot to strike the ball because the goalie will have much more time to react to stop a shot from a striker that is far away from the net. Using the inside of your foot is a bit more accurate but is not as powerful as using the bone of your foot. The goalie will have more time to react to a shot that is struck with the inside of your foot than with the bone of your foot.

Now, keep in mind that this form is for when the goalie is in the net. If the goalie has come out of the net and you are on a counterattack, it is appropriate to use the inside of your foot to pop the ball over them. When there are defenders in the 18-yard box, you are shooting from outside, and the goalie is standing in the net, then make sure you are using the bone of your foot. **Now, if you are close to the net, say at the penalty area or even**

closer, you want to use the inside of your foot because it is going to provide you more accuracy on your shot. At this point, the goalie will have very little time to react, so you want to focus more on the accuracy of your shot than its power. Also, consider the chapter in this book on shooting the ball with the outside of your foot for an additional and very effective way to strike the ball out of the air when the ball is directly in front of you.

Chapter 16

Fast Restarts

Restarts are where the ball has gone out of bounds or has been awarded to a team because of a foul. The ball must be sent back into play for the game to continue. **Restarts are perfect opportunities for you and your team to catch the other side off guard.** More than likely, the other team will take a few seconds to travel to the correct positions to defend the ball coming back into play. Frequently, soccer players on both sides will not be hustling hard enough to be in the area that they need to be in during a restart and take a few seconds for a mental break too. Being able to place the ball quickly back into play for a "fast restart" is a great way to give your team a slight advantage. Keep in mind that if it is late in a game and your team is winning, you generally want to be very slow with your restarts unless you see a perfect restart opportunity for a quick goal. However, if it is early in a game, your team is tied, or your team is losing, it is an opportune time for you to have a fast restart.

Use the quick restart to effectively create a situation that would not have been available had the play not been stopped. **Therefore, it is important to emphasize that as soon as a ball goes out of bounds**

and it is your team's ball, sprint to the ball. If the ball went out and is now a throw-in, corner kick, goal kick, or free kick, then immediately look for the other person on your team that is paying attention too. There is often only one or two players on a team that are mentally sharp enough to look for a quick pass to place the other team in a dangerous position. This teammate is the player on your team that does not take a few second break that the rest of the players on the field tend to do. This person is hungry for the ball and confident in turning a chance into a goal. In a fast restart, you can easily send the ball back into play to beat several players that you would have either had to dribble or pass around if you chose not to have a fast restart.

As an example, I use fast restarts to my advantage when it is going to be a corner kick. I will run as fast as I can to grab the ball, place the ball on the quarter circle near the flag, and then immediately look for the person that is making their delayed run into the box or is wide open checking to the corner flag that I can pass to quickly. A quick corner is useful because the defense is likely not set up to defend the corner kick and many of them are not even going to be looking at the ball initially when you go to kick it into the 18-yard box. **Before the game has even started, I have communicated to my teammates my intentions in a game when I am passed the ball, after**

it has gone out of bounds. They know to quickly become open so that I will pass the ball to them.

The same holds true on a goal kick that your team is taking. Granted the ball has not been kicked 40 yards out of bounds, the goalie must immediately grab the ball and place it in the 6-yard box. It does not have to be perfectly set on the line. Taking too much time to set down the ball for a goal kick is something where many goalies make a mistake. The goalie will set it perfectly and then look for the pass to a teammate. What they should do is to look for the pass and only set it perfectly on the 6-yard line if there are no quick restart options. **If you are on a team that can pass well and maintains possession, then look for a quick pass out of the 18-yard box. If your team has a dominant forward or is much better off with the ball in the other team's half, then the goalie should look for that one forward that is paying attention and pass the ball to him or her when they do not have many defenders nearby.**

One of the most exciting things about fast restarts is that it does not take good soccer skills to utilize them. It just takes quick thinking and at least one other teammate that is paying attention. Bring this up with teammates in practice or before a game regarding your intentions if the ball goes out of bounds. Otherwise, when you are in a game and a teammate did not see an opportunity for a fast restart, give constructive feedback to your teammate by saying "hey, next time please do... [insert what you needed them to do to make a fast restart a reality]." Another exciting thing about fast restarts is that you do not necessarily even need the best cross into the box or the best pass from your own six-yard box. If you have a quick restart, the other team will have accidentally given you much more room for error, as long as you play quickly because their lack of awareness for a few seconds increases the chance that the shot goes in, the pass is completed, or the throw-in is to an open player.

The reverse holds true too. **Your team needs to pay attention at all times and be very aware of fast restarts as well because it is incredibly demotivating and can indeed halt your team's momentum when the other team scores what you may consider a "cheap" goal because you were not paying attention.** Remember, how the ball goes in (as long as you are not cheating) does not matter. It is great for your team to score a cheap goal because a goal is a goal. If it means you are scoring a cheap goal because the other side was not paying attention, then that is the other team's fault for having the few seconds where they were taking a mental and physical rest. Fast restarts are another possible weakness of an opponent's defense that might not be there otherwise in the ordinary course of play.

Chapter 17

Toe Pokes/Toe Blows

When you first start playing soccer, you instinctively start off kicking the ball with your toe. You are quickly told that using a toe poke/toe blow is incorrect and that you should be using the bone of your foot to shoot. In fact, many of my trainees make fun of other trainees when they kick the ball with their toe. The trainees have been so conditioned that using their toe is incorrect, that they are confident enough to tease others who use it. However, after playing soccer with that limiting belief for the last 15 years, I have come across three instances I can remember that have entirely shifted my mindset over the last few years.

First, when I was playing in a scrimmage against another team, the other team's coach had stopped his player after an attempt to score. **The coach pulled the player and told him "when you are that close to the net, do not be afraid to toe poke/toe blow the ball if that is the only way you can take a shot. A shot with your toe is going to be a lot better than no shot at all."** For me, the other team's coach drove home the message that taking more shots is going to result in more goals, even if they are not perfect shots. The chance may end up being a lucky and accurate shot, the goalie may mishandle the ball resulting in a goal, or the goalie may give up an easy rebound for yourself or a teammate to shoot the ball in the back of the net.

Second, it was a handful of years ago that I was watching the El Clásico between the world's two largest soccer clubs: Barcelona and Real Madrid. The game ended in a draw because of Cristiano Ronaldo's goal. The average soccer fan watching simply saw that the ball went in the net. However, on closer inspection of the goal, the ball was played a little too far in front of Cristiano Ronaldo for him to shoot any other way than to use a toe poke/toe blow. **This example points out that you can extend your leg further in front of you to reach the ball by using your toes to kick the ball, which means that you can reach further out and allow yourself to take more shots over your career when you understand that using your toe to shoot is acceptable.** Keep in mind that when you are within 10 yards of the net, you do not need the most accurate shots because the goalie is not going to have a lot of time to react. Make sure that you take a shot to test the keeper to increase your chances of scoring and ultimately winning the game.

Third, I was watching a highlight reel of outstanding goals. I can only recall Ronaldinho's goal from the video that was several minutes long. Ronaldinho's goal was when he was still playing for Barcelona. On the YouTube video highlight reel, he scored from just outside the 18-yard box. He was standing still for a few seconds looking for a pass. The defender gave him as much time as he wanted as the defender felt he had stopped Ronaldinho from advancing with the ball or being able to shoot. The defender was standing in front of Ronaldinho and was waiting for him to make a move when Ronaldinho decided to toe blow the ball, which resulted in him scoring a goal. If you have watched any of Ronaldinho's highlight videos before, then you have likely seen this goal and can imagine it right now.

A key takeaway from this is that using a toe poke/toe blow creates deception that allows you to take a shot more efficiently. The defender was not expecting Ronaldinho's shot with his toes. The defender figured that it would be unrealistic for Ronaldinho to have any power on a shot given that he was standing still. The defender had it in his mind that he would either pass the ball or shoot a weak shot that the goalie could easily stop. However, Ronaldinho being the cheeky player that he is thought of a fancy and effective way to make the best out of the possible options he had available. He sought an opportunity to improve his team's chances of winning by toe poking/toe blowing the ball and took complete advantage of it. He was close enough to the net (on the 18-yard box) to have a toe blow be a viable option. If he were any further from the net, it would not have been reasonable to use his toe to strike the ball.

Therefore, by using the toe of your foot to shoot during appropriate game situations, it allows for three things that using the bone of your foot often does not:

1. **Provides an additional way for you to take a shot.** Make sure to strike the ball just below the center of the middle of the ball when doing a toe poke/toe blow.

2. **Allows you to extend your leg so that you can take more shots.**

3. **It is very deceptive to use a toe blow** because most goalies and defenders do not think that people will use their toe to kick a soccer ball, so it is misleading. You do not have to extend at the hip (only at the knee) as you would with the form for a driven shot, so it takes less time to take a shot, which makes it very easy to be disguised.

In fact, I have a great friend previously mentioned in this book that plays soccer with me. He is a "maestro" when it comes to shooting with every part of his foot. He uses the inside of his foot, the bone of his foot, the outside of his foot, and he uses toe pokes/toe blows too. What is even more exciting is that he can do this with both feet. His versatility in shooting allows him to catch the defender and the goalie off guard to score efficiently. His resourcefulness in the way that he shoots makes nearly every situation when he is close to the net a shooting situation.

Chapter 18

2v2s

A 2v2 is a typical scenario that soccer players will often find themselves in during a game where there is a portion of the field where the only people that are a part of the play are two players from each team. **A quality defense will attempt to bring both of the attacking players as close together as possible.** Also, they will try to slow the forward momentum to allow other players on their team to come back to provide additional support. Slowing a forward's momentum makes it much easier to defend.

Think about it, if the defenders can move the two attackers closer together, then there is an increased chance for an opportunity for the defenders to have four feet swinging at the ball to attempt to poke the ball away or to dispossess the attackers instead of just two feet. **Even if the defense does not steal the ball right away, they are successful when they can slow the attacker's progress up the field just enough for teammates to come back into position and help defend.** Making quick progress in 1v1s, 2v1s, and 2v2s, so that the defenders are not successful is why it is essential that you attack with speed.

Generally, you will want to create several yards of space, so that if the person with the ball elects not to pass the ball but to dribble their defender instead, they will not have to beat an additional defender as well. Excitingly, if your teammate does decide to pass the ball, you being further from your teammate will increase the chance of you finding a lane to travel in behind the defense to make it easy for you to have an open shot on net with only the goalie there to stop it. Keep in mind that a 2v2 is very situational. A 2v2 in your own third of the field is very different than a 2v2 when you are in the attacking third. When you are in your own third of the field, you definitely do not want to dribble. Furthermore, unless you have a clear pass, you may consider just booting the ball up the field to avoid a forward from the other team attempting to steal the ball from you. Simply booting the ball up the field will buy your team some time to reorganize. For the rest of this chapter, I will be referring to a 2v2 when you are in the attacking third of the field where you are working to score a goal.

When you are the person without the ball in a 2v2, there are two predominant options for you. First, make a phenomenal run that allows for an easy pass from your teammate that sets you up to attack the goalie without having to beat a defender. **A tip that works well is to**

take your first two to three steps in the wrong direction with the hope that the defender will start to cut you off in that direction. A few steps in the wrong direction will provide you space to explode in the direction you actually want to go.

The second option is to make a run that pulls both of the defenders towards you, which makes it easier for the attacker to find an open lane with the ball to take a high probability shot on net. To accomplish this, start by running behind the first defender that is guarding your teammate who has the ball, but in front of the defender that is guarding you. A run that splits the defenders will naturally pull both defenders towards you because the defender that is defending your teammate will not be able to fully see you and will step a bit towards your direction looking to cut off the pass. The second defender is responsible for marking you and staying close enough to you to decrease your chances of being a threat. Drawing both defenders toward you allows the striker to attack the space in the direction from which you came. This second option often does not involve you scoring the goal and potentially not even the assist if you were not the person that passed it to your teammate.

However, it is critical to be the player that is willing to sacrifice your own stats at times to make

sure that the ultimate goal of the game is being met, which is for your team to win. It is one of those unselfish things that you can do to achieve your team's objective of winning and ultimately is a reason why it is included in this book because this is an important topic for you and your team to finish and score in games. Also, you may not have been included on the stat sheet for that specific goal, but let's be honest, when your team scores several goals against its opponent, their spirits and energy will start to become crushed. This will inherently reduce their effort, which will make it easier for you to score later in the game.

If you are the person in a 2v2 with the ball, your best two options are very similar to the options of the teammate who does not have the ball. Again, it cannot be stressed enough that 2v2s are situational, but this scenario is for the most common 2v2 that you will be in where both defenders are in front of both attackers.

Your first option as the person with the ball in a 2v2 is to pass the ball if your teammate is making a quality run into space that is feasible for you to make a pass. If your teammate is not making a good run that allows for a relatively easy pass for you, then reconsider passing because if you pass the ball: 1. You have to complete the pass. 2. Your teammate has to take a quality first touch. 3.

Then, your teammate must shoot the ball. Yes, your teammate could also take a one-time shot that would allow their first touch to be their shot. **Conversely, if you hold onto the ball, you take the passing component out that potentially can lead to an inaccurate pass on your part or a poor run on your teammate's part.** Here, you only need to rely on your ability to find a little bit of space to shoot the ball, while expecting your other teammate to score any rebounds just as you expect to score them too.

The second option is for you to shoot without making a pass to your teammate. Use your judgment in the situation to know if you can rely on your own passing skills, whether the defense is giving you space, and your ability to shoot versus your teammate's ability to shoot. Though this is not the easiest thing to do at full speed in a game situation, it is something that comes much more naturally with time. **If your pass will result in a shot that is just as difficult as the one you will take, you are better off not passing because then you are just adding more potential for error.**

Lastly, a key point always to remember is to be explosive in these types of situations to catch the defenders that are a little bit flat-footed. By being able to accelerate into space very quickly, you will increase the chances of your team scoring, whether it be your teammate or you that scores.

Chapter 19

The Rebounding Mentality

Often, being able to turn a rebound into a goal is what separates a good team from a great team. **In soccer, it usually is just one goal that separates the winners from the losers or the team that won from the team that merely tied its opponent.** It is essential that you and your teammates are on the same page when it comes to scoring rebounds. As you begin to adopt the ideas in this book and really increase the volume of shots being taken, you will naturally have a lot more opportunities for placing rebounds into the back of the net. Rebounds are generally easy to shoot into the back of the net, but you have to make sure you plan this as a team. If this is not communicated properly and every midfielder and forward is looking to score a rebound, then there will be very few players in position to stop the other team. Specifically, if all the forwards and midfielders are pushing too far forward, then it makes it very easy for the other team to start a counterattack in the opposite direction.

Let us play out a scenario where we have the center midfielder shooting. If you have both forwards, both outside midfielders, and the other center midfielder attacking the net for a rebound assuming that a center midfielder took a shot, then that leaves only a few people remaining for defense. Specifically, the person that shot the ball and the four defenders are left to defend many of the other team's players that will start sprinting up the field towards your goal, expecting a pass from their keeper, when their goalie is able to collect a shot quickly.

Therefore, it is recommended that a team's forwards are always in search of rebounds because for a good portion of the game they are not involved in the action. Think about it, if the ball is on your half of the field and the other team has possession, there is a good chance that your team's forwards might jog a bit here and there, but they are hardly utilized until their team has the ball. Therefore, a forward will generally have the stamina to take on the additional workload of being a ball hawk who is continuously looking for rebounds. Again, these examples are very dependent on the scenario, so use your judgment and learn from watching and playing the game. More experience will lead to better results.

Determining which players should be running towards the goalie after a shot with hopes to score a rebound depends mostly on the quality of the shot taken and the quality of the goalkeeper. Good shots are much harder to catch than bad shots. Ineffective goalies give up a lot more rebounds than high-quality goalkeepers. **As**

such, before the game starts, have one person designated on your team or one member of the coaching staff watch the other goalie in warm-ups if the other team's goalie is someone that you have not played against before. Have the designated person communicate the goalie's level of skill to their team before the game starts. Implement the information as part of the team's game plan because a good team will look for the others team's weaknesses and exploit them without being too far away from their own playing style in the process.

When you are playing against a good goalkeeper, only have your forwards crash the net after a shot. Just using your forwards in this situation will not only give your team's forwards potential to shoot any loose balls in the back of the net, but it keeps your outside midfielders in a more defensive mindset and position to easily cover the other team's outside midfielders should the goalie swiftly collect the ball and look to help his team create a quick counterattack. When it is observed that the goalkeeper on the other team is average or below average, then consider having have both your forwards and outside midfielders crash the net to place any rebounds into the back of the net.

Keep in mind that this is very situational and can change with each play. **If you are a forward taking a shot, then you should definitely be looking for a rebound because you will have the best idea of where the rebound will end up from your shot.** It is not recommending that the center midfielders crash the net to score a rebound because the opposing team is going to be more dangerous if they are allowed space for a counterattack up the middle of the field than they would be with a counterattack up one of the sidelines of the field.

Next, when approaching rebounds, remember that an okay shot is much better than no shot. Too many players think they need to have a lot of space, time, the right angle to the net, and be on the right spot of the field before it is appropriate to shoot. Keep in mind that we are talking about rebounds here, so you are generally going to be pretty close to the net if you do come upon a rebound. **In times of chaos in front of the net, this is when the goalie is most likely going to make a mistake.** Therefore, you should be sure to really test the other team's goalkeeper. If you come upon a rebound, use whatever part of your foot you need to take the ball back in the direction of the net to increase your chances of scoring.

Having good form is obviously preferred when you take the shots off of a rebound, but **perfect form at this point is not the most important thing when you are only a few yards away from the net.** Depending on the rebound that is given up, the other team's goalie might not be positioned in front of a second shot at all. These instances are when you especially need to make sure that you are the first one to the ball because if you are, you will have an empty net to shoot on and an easy goal for your team to celebrate. Always have the mindset of chasing rebounds, especially if you are a forward and if you observe the goalie making mistakes. Also, always be active on your toes (the balls of your feet) and be ready to explode in whatever direction necessary to be the first one to the ball.

For any opposing goalie that does not seem very good, make sure the forwards and outside midfielders are crashing the net after shots, when feasible. Do not expect to effectively crash the net if you are 30 yards away from the net when your teammate shoots the ball. If the goalie seems skillful in warm-ups, then only have forwards crashing the net because they will have the capacity and the energy to be the first one to rebounds. However, make sure that your outside midfielders are looking to prevent a counterattack and not overcommitting to rebounds that probably will not be there. Keep in mind that this is for shots that occur during regular gameplay, not for free kicks from set pieces. **Also, consider the field conditions on which you are playing. Generally, there is going to be fewer rebounds when it is a perfect 75°F sunny day with no wind than there will be on a day where the field is wet, which makes the ball slippery and easy for the goalie to mishandle.**

Furthermore, consider the person shooting. If one of the best shooters on your team is shooting, expect a rebound if the ball does not go in, but if someone that is not a good shooter is shooting many yards away from the net, then the goalie will very likely be able to recover the shot without giving up a rebound. Also, remember that taking a shot is very important to test the keeper and an okay shot off a rebound is still probably going to be a goal. Notice that when you watch players on television at the highest levels across the world, oftentimes their goals are not the result of perfect form on a wonderful shot from 30 yards out or from them dribbling past eight or nine players. Their goal is a result of them being in the right place at the right time.

Yes, being in the right place at the right time does take a little bit of luck but also takes skill to make sure you are consistently at or near the spot on the field that gives you the best chance for collecting

a rebound. Remember that a goal from a rebound counts for as many points, as a fancier goal. If you can dribble an entire team like Lionel Messi or take a rocket of a shot from 35 yards out like Cristiano Ronaldo, that is fine, but if you don't have those skills, then make yourself useful in other areas such as scoring rebounds. At times, I need to remember this too, as I tend to look to accumulate most of my goals from shots or dribbling many defenders. Do not only rely on your ability to shoot or dribble. Scoring off of rebounds will also increase the number of options you have to score. This will increase the amount that you can help your team achieve its goal of winning each and every game.

Chapter 20

Penalty Kick Ideas

Disclaimer: If you are not the first or second option on your team selected when a penalty kick is awarded, then it is highly advised to limit how often you practice penalty kicks. Instead, focus on practicing the other areas in this book and once you begin producing more goals, then come back to this chapter.

I write the disclaimer because only a few times in your career, if ever, will you ever have the ball perfectly stopped on the penalty line/dot with all the time in the world to approach the ball at a pace that is comfortable to you. It just hardly ever happens, so it is not the most productive thing to spend your practice time on unless your coach would select you to take one in a game. **Keep in mind that a significant portion of the practice time should be spent on the things that are necessary to do in a game.** Things like passing, dribbling, shooting a driven shot with the ball rolling, or being able to defend. With that idea firmly engrained in your mind, let us move on to the best practices for a penalty shot. A great striker will always have two penalty shot placements that they are comfortable taking. One shot that goes to the right side of the net and one shot that goes to the left side of the net. **Things to consider on the form for both of your options on penalty kicks:**

1. Have the same run-up/approach to the ball.

2. Have the same foot placement next to the ball with your plant foot, so you are not revealing any information to the goalie.

3. Driven shots are preferred.

4. Once you have perfected steps 1-3, consider picking your head up a bit, to see which way the goalkeeper is going.

First, having the same run-up for both of your penalty shots is essential because as you start to advance in your soccer career, other teams will watch games that you play in and try to obtain an edge on you. Knowing which way you shoot on penalty kicks is one of those edges. Therefore, if you can master two penalty shots where you start from the same spot on the field to approach the ball, you will not be giving any "signs" or "tells" of what side of the net you will be shooting towards.

Second, your plant foot is ideally positioned the same whether you are going to the right or the left with your shot. **Preferably, your plant foot is pointed right down the middle of the net because the goalie will likely assume that if it is pointed to the right, you will be shooting to the right or if it is pointed to the left, you will be shooting to the left.** Therefore, a plant foot pointed straight at the keeper is quite deceptive and tricky for them.

Third, driven shots, as opposed to shots with the inside of your foot, your toe, or the outside of your foot are better because they are much more powerful. Even if the goalie gets a hand on the ball, they are unlikely to stop the ball because it will be too powerful and deflect off their hand while still ending up in the back of their net. **Furthermore, driven shots travel faster than the other types of shots, which means the goalie has less time to react.** Less time to react is great news for the person taking the penalty because even if the shot is not perfectly placed, but is still within the frame of the net, then there is a very high chance it will still end up in the back the net.

An example of a prominent player who only takes driven shots on penalty kicks is Jamie Vardy of the Leicester City F.C. English Premier League team. If you watched the 2015–16 Leicester City F.C. season where the Foxes (their mascot) came up from nowhere to win one of the most highly contested league titles in all of sports, you would have seen more than a handful of Jamie Vardy's penalty kicks. (I had him on my fantasy soccer team, so I surely saw them.) Jamie's objective with every penalty shot and nearly every shot taken in the game as well as to drive the ball as hard as possible when shooting. He did this exceptionally well in their title campaign by striking low and driven shots into the back of the net to lead his team to the title and to be his team's leading goal scorer.

Fourth, when and only when you have the first three mastered, **consider practicing the advanced technique of looking where the goalie is diving to shoot in the opposite direction.** If you can place a driven shot in the direction away from where the keeper is diving, you will likely be unstoppable as a penalty kicker. Being able to kick the ball while focusing on the keeper's movements does take a considerable amount of practice to master and should mostly be practiced against a qualified keeper, so that you may begin to pick up the tendencies a goalie has when they attempt to save your penalty kick. Keep in mind that you will only have a split second to judge where they will be diving, which is why this is an advanced technique. This technique was told to me by a friend and soccer player, Tom Catalano, a former semi-pro forward who hardly missed a penalty kick in his 20-year playing career.

In conclusion, have two penalty kick shots that you practice and are able to master. One that is placed to the right side of the net and the other that is placed towards the left side of the net. Approach the ball the same way for both shots. Point the toe of your plant foot directly down the center of the net. Lastly, once you are comfortable using a driven shot, then use it for your penalty kicks to increase the chances that your penalty kick will result in a goal for your team. When it comes to being awarded penalty kicks, avoid flopping in the box to have a penalty called in favor of your team. However, if you are fouled and have no chance to maintain possession of the ball, then fall. Make the referee decide because if you do not drop, they will NOT call a penalty kick, even if you were fouled.

Chapter 21

Bicycle Kicks & the Crossbar Challenge

In soccer, there are few things that are actually believed to be bad to work on as a soccer player. The two that stand out most for me and that immediately come to mind are practicing bicycle kicks and playing the crossbar challenge.

Bicycle kicks are one of those things that look fabulous and will often make it onto ESPN SportsCenter's top 10 plays. Also, it is true that bicycle kicks are things you remember for your entire playing career. **However, bicycle kicks are not efficient to spend practice time on.** A situation in the game where the ball is overhead slightly further than the where you can jump to head the ball, but where you will have the space to use the exact foot that you have practiced with to take a shot on the net is very impractical and only happens a few times in a season at best.

Therefore, as a soccer player, you want to be consistent about practicing the things that you will encounter every single game. **Make sure that you have those perfected and then work on things that occasionally happen.** If you have all those things perfected, then you are probably playing at the highest level of soccer right now. If you do not have those things perfected, start with the basics and work your way up to skills that will less frequently be needed in a game. A bicycle kick is not a basic thing to do nor is it something that you will really ever need to do in soccer. My recommendation is not to spend the practice time working on bicycle kicks and spend more time working on shooting, passing, dribbling, or even headers off a corner or cross.

Similarly, the crossbar challenge is something that is often detrimental to a player's ability to shoot and finish. The crossbar challenge is the game where you stand outside of the 18-yard box and shoot to hit the crossbar. The player that is able to do it wins and those that are unable to lose. Players will often shoot toward the middle of the crossbar to increase their chances of hitting the crossbar because if they are a little bit off and shoot the ball left or right, they may still hit the crossbar. **But think about it, you are practicing shooting the ball at a target that is not the back of the net and it is a portion of the net that you generally would not want to shoot at in a game.**

The middle of the crossbar is a more easily covered spot by the goalkeeper than is the side netting.

Remember that you play the way you practice and if you are partaking in the crossbar challenge, you are practicing something that you would never hope to do in a game. I can hear your potential opposing viewpoint already "but I am working on my accuracy."

It is understandable that you are working on your accuracy, but it is being accurate in a way that is not productive to the accuracy you would want in a game. As mentioned previously in this book, most of your shots should be low and driven, not high and lofted. **Therefore, practicing a shot with form that is detrimental to your ability to score is an ineffective use of your time.** You are literally spending time practicing not to score. Instead, my recommendation is to play the "side net" challenge. Instead of shooting from outside of the 18-yard box and aiming to hit the crossbar, shoot from the outside of the 18-yard box and see who can shoot the ball into the side netting without the ball touching the ground. This game is just as fun and is more practical for real game experience. In fact, to make it even more realistic, require all the shots from outside the 18-yard box to be with a soccer ball that is rolling and not stopped. In conclusion, this book is all about helping you score. Use the information in this book to take your game to the next level.

Soccer Dribbling & Foot Skills:

A Step-by-Step Guide on How to Dribble Past the Other Team

Chapter 1

How to Dribble Effectively

In soccer, being a confident dribbler is key to advancing your abilities as a soccer player. If you work towards and become a soccer player that can consistently move the ball up the field with your foot skills, you will be a very productive member of any team. To dribble correctly, ensure that you are dribbling with speed. **To dribble with speed, have your toes down and in, pushing off the ground using the balls of your foot (i.e., the portion of the bottom of your foot just below the toes).** If someone ever asks you to stand on your tippy toes, he or she is really asking you to stand on your toes and balls of your feet.

The reason a soccer player does not want to be flat-footed when dribbling is for the same reason a soccer player does not want to run flat-footed. The soccer player will go too slowly and effective dribblers use their agility provided from being on their toes to beat defenders. If you ever watch the fastest soccer players or even the sprinters in the Olympics, you will notice that they run on the balls of their feet to fully engage their calf muscles to be as quick as possible.

Sadly, running on the balls of my feet was not something I figured out until college. In fact, to practice running properly, I would run from class to class focusing exclusively on running with proper form to make sure I could transition to being a faster runner on the field. The other people at the university thought I was a bit odd, given that I was the only person that anyone ever saw running outside of a gym or field, but I was determined to become a faster and more explosive runner. Being able to meet two objectives at once makes it a lot easier to improve and grow more rapidly. In this example, I had to go to class (objective one) and I wanted to improve my speed and running form (objective two).

Getting back to the dribbling form, having the positioning of your foot with your toes down and in, while curling just your toes up (not your ankle) will allow you to essentially **create a "scooper" with your foot** to ensure that you have an accurate push of the ball every time you make contact with it. This form is ideal because it allows you to use the same running form as if you did not have the ball while maintaining the correct contact with the ball using the bone of the top of your foot. Proper form when dribbling guarantees precision with every touch and enough power to dribble the ball with speed.

Pushing the ball with the inside of your foot forces you to point your foot outwards. An outward pointed foot slows down your speed drastically when running, which makes dribbling with the inside of your foot unreasonable.

Dribbling with the outside of your foot points your toes too far inward, which makes it equally as unreasonable to dribble with the outside of the foot. **Dribbling with your toes down and slightly pointed in is the happy medium to allow you to dribble quickly while running.**

Also, when you go to push the ball when the defender is very close to you, do not just push it straight on the ground past the defender. Instead, flick the ball up in the air a little bit. Flicking the ball will give you an increased probability of dribbling by the defender because the ball is more likely to travel past the defender by going over their foot. **Use a slight flick in your push after doing a skill, like a jab step or a scissor, to move the ball over any outstretched legs.** If you flick it, so the ball slightly bounces, you can continue to dribble without any wasted time. Furthermore, flicking the ball past the defender's foot, so that it jumps a bit, will allow you to hit a rocket of a shot. You can strike a powerful shot with a bouncing ball because you can make complete contact with the ball while the ball is bouncing and there is no friction between the ball and the ground that also slows a shot.

Chapter 2

Dribbling with Speed vs. Speed Dribbling

Dribbling for many players consists of taking a touch of the ball every step. A touch every step does not often lead to dribbling with speed and is not efficient in many situations. **Dribbling with speed involves taking a touch only when necessary, but relying heavily on bigger touches and your speed to travel faster in less time.** Understanding this is so critical because you are faster without the ball than you are with the ball. Therefore, the more touches you take with the ball, the slower you will be.

An example I often use with my trainees is that I will tell them that I am going to travel 10 yards in two different ways. The first way I proceed to show them is to take five touches while dribbling the 10 yards. The trainees are then able to observe the time it takes for this option. Next, I travel the 10 yards with one touch. They see that it is two to three times quicker because less touches take less time. Take Gareth Bale who has played for Tottenham, Real Madrid, and the Wales National Team. He understands that his strength is his speed, so he is unafraid to push the ball far out in front of him, which allows his legs to really run.

Therefore, when traveling with the ball in a game or practice, it is essential to take bigger touches that allow you to run after the ball when you are attacking. **When you have space on the field, travel through the area as quickly as possible with only one or two touches. Therefore, dribbling with speed means that you are judging the situation and taking an appropriate amount of touches based on the space you have available.**

Dribbling with speed effectively allows you to bait players on the other team. When you push the ball out in front of you as you are attacking forward, larger pushes bait defenders in. Specifically, pushing the ball several yards away gives defenders the hope that they will be able to intercept the ball or slide tackle it away. A professional that does this very well is Cristiano Ronaldo. He effectively uses his speed and large dribbles in order to bait defenders into over-committing themselves for the ball, which allows him to have a last-second push of the ball away from the opposition.

As previously mentioned, dribbling with speed is pushing the ball many steps forward before taking another touch whereas **speed dribbling is taking a touch every step, but every step is a full running stride to ensure you are traveling as fast as possible with the ball**. An example of a professional that does this exceptionally well is Lionel Messi. Messi is outstanding at being able to run basically as fast while speed dribbling as he is taking one large touch into space and sprinting after the ball. His ability to dribble others is out of this world and he is very efficient in the skills he uses, something that will be talked more about later in this book.

Speed dribbling is something to be practiced so that it can be perfected. It is essential to find the balance between the control needed to run with a ball, but being able to run at the same speed without the ball. Speed dribbling gives you the ability to take a touch with every step, which is vital to be able to adjust your run with the ball as the defenders reveal what they are doing to take the ball from you. **If a defender lunges or slides for the ball, you are more easily able to do a skill to avoid the oncoming defender than you would be able to with dribbles that travel a significant distance in one push.**

Soccer players looking to advance their game will work to become great at **dribbling with speed (taking a large touch to cover several yards with one touch) and speed dribbling (being able to sprint while pushing the ball with every step of the foot that is dribbling the ball)**. Most players learn speed dribbling, but do not learn about dribbling with speed. Combine these both and raise your abilities past those of your opponents and even your teammates.

Chapter 3

How to React Based on a Defender's Stance

When attacking a defender, do you ever wonder how you should read their body language to make it easier for you to dribble past them? **Well, based on their positioning in front of you, in addition to their stance (which way their hips are facing), you can determine what direction they are looking to force you to travel.** Additionally, it can reveal if they lack the correct defending technique. A good defender will force you in the direction they want you to go. A great attacker will go in the direction that gives him or her the highest probability of success. A great attacker will likely be able to go both ways, but he or she will want to assess the situation and determine which direction will make it easier for him or her to strike a shot or complete a pass.

In the first book of this Understand Soccer Series, *Soccer Training: A Step-by-Step Guide on 14 Topics for Intelligent Soccer Players, Coaches, and Parents*, we discussed what an appropriate stance for a defender is. A defender that wants you to go to your right should have their right foot slightly in front of their left foot so that their hips are pointing diagonally to the left. The defender should not be directly in front of the attacker but slightly off to the attackers left side creating more space for the attacker to dribble up the field to the right. The reverse applies when a defender wants to give you space to your left. Keep in mind that not all defenders position themselves properly. **If a defender is directly in front of you and has their hips turned to the right, attack to the left.** If they have their hips turned to the left, then attack to the right because it will take more time and it will be slower for them to transition from their hips pointing one way to turn and sprint in the other direction.

Now that you understand correct positioning for a defender let us consider options when attacking. **If a defender gives you space to your opposite foot, take it.** This is granted you are comfortable shooting or passing with your opposite foot. If the defender is directly in front of you and turned to the right or the left, attack the opposite direction they are facing, all other things being equal. If the defender's hips are pointed directly at you and not turned to the right or left at all, then attack in the direction that will give you an easier shot on net or a pass to a teammate. If they have square hips this is one of the easiest times for you to do a nutmeg. However, see the chapter on nutmegs to find out why it is still not the best idea to pursue. If the defender has an additional supporting defender, they would want to be pushing you into that supporting defender.

To conclude, as a dribbler looking to take advantage of a defender's stance, attack the direction the defender is not facing if they are positioned directly in front of you. If the defender is slightly off to one side and not straight in front of you, then attack in the direction they are giving you more space to dribble in. **However, if they are forcing you to your opposite foot and you are not yet experienced enough to use it, then consider trying to attack to your dominant foot, knowing that you are making it more difficult for yourself, given that you cannot use both feet.** Some moves to accomplish this are the jab step, scissor, or shot fake using the inside of the foot to help create space to enable you to travel to your dominant foot, which are all discussed in great detail in later chapters of this book. An excellent example of this was the UEFA Champions League match of Barcelona versus Bayern Munich, where Lionel Messi effectively attacked Jerome Boateng's stance. The result was a goal for Barcelona and a very memorable Boateng tripping over himself in the process.

Chapter 4

Tier 1 – Jab Steps, Self-Passes, & Shot Fakes

Bruce Lee, the famous martial artist and philosopher, once said: "I fear not the man who has practiced 10,000 kicks once, but I fear the man who has practiced one kick 10,000 times." What he is saying is do not settle with being okay by dabbling with many skills in many different areas. He recommends you to be the best in only one thing. **When it comes to soccer, it means pick one skill for each of the different circumstances in a game that you would encounter while dribbling the soccer ball and develop those skills and ONLY those.**

Therefore, the BIG 3 skills that are recommended for all soccer players to develop are the jab step, self-pass, and shot fake. If you subscribed to the UnderstandSoccer.com email list, then this chapter will look familiar. If not, it is highly recommended to subscribe to it for tips, tricks, tweaks, and techniques emailed to you about one time per week. Also, you will have updates on the next book in the series and I have been known to give away books for free.

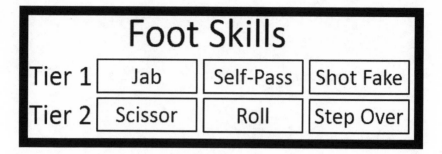

Foot Skills			
Tier 1	Jab	Self-Pass	Shot Fake
Tier 2	Scissor	Roll	Step Over

First, the jab step goes by many names: the shoulder drop, the fake, the fake and take, the feint, the body feint, or whatever else you would like to call it. The name is not essential, but mastering the skill is crucial. This skill is by far the best attacking move to use when a defender is backpedaling and you are looking to dribble by him or her. Now, keep in mind that any skill is just to make the defender off balance for a split second. A split second where the defender thinks that you are going in one direction when you intend to take the ball in another direction. However, it is the explosive change of speed after the skill that buys you more time than performing the jab step with the appropriate form. **A good jab step involves the ball starting outside your shoulder and turning your toe down and in to make it look like you will push/dribble the ball.**

Some soccer players may prefer to use the scissor or the step over in this game situation. **Yet, the jab step allows you to make no contact whatsoever with the**

ball and does not require any extra body positioning that involves additional steps similar to that of a scissor. Additionally, this is not the correct time at all to be doing a step over. A correctly performed scissor requires that you step your plant foot past the ball so that you can turn at the hips, which will allow the ball to roll through your legs while the defender is off balance, allowing you to push the ball and attack in the opposite direction that you had faked going. The extra step in a scissor to correctly have your body positioned past the ball takes extra time versus a jab step.

Let us use a very well-known player to demonstrate this further - Lionel Messi. Some would argue that he is or is not the best soccer player, however, there is not much of an argument when someone says he is the best dribbler in the world. **When you watch him, it does not look like he is doing a bunch of skills to dribble past the defenders since it looks so effortless. However, upon further inspection, you will see that he is using the most efficient skills, which he has perfected.** He uses the most efficient skills to score more goals, tally more assists, and increase the chance that his team wins.

Again, this is not to say that the other skills are bad, it is just that they are not as likely to work. Think about it this way, if you do a jab step and you have a 90% success rate, whereas when you perform a scissor, you have an 80% success rate. **The jab step is a better option because you will have a higher percentage of successes with that skill because it takes less time than the scissor.** An example of the quality of the jab step is that during one of the previous Next Level Training soccer summer camps that I was a trainer at, there was a girl that followed my advice in a drill that we were doing. The drill was simply 1v1s and you had to travel to the other side of the grid for a point. The player, Emily, did the same jab step nine times in a row and it worked every single time.

Next, the self-pass is a very effective skill when the defender is reaching in for the ball. Anytime he or she is reaching towards you to take the ball away, it naturally means their momentum is going towards you and your momentum is going in the opposite direction. This means you do not need to fake the ball one way and take it another way when the opposing player is lunging toward the ball. Simply move the ball out of the way. The self-pass is also known as an "L", an Iniesta, or a la croqueta. It is as easy as passing the ball from one foot to the other, straight across the defender's body. Notice that it said "across the defender's body" and not across your own body. Going "across the defender's body" is critical because we do not want the ball traveling diagonally in relation to the defender because then it moves the ball closer to them, which makes it easier for them to steal the ball than if we moved the ball straight across him or her. Remember, the first portion of the self-pass is the bottom of an "L," which will make it a lot easier to dribble the ball by the defender.

Lastly, you can perform a shot fake in various ways. You can perform your shot fake using a Cruyff, a step on step out, a jump turn, a V pull back, an outside of the foot cut, or an inside of the foot cut. Each of which has an appropriate time to use in a game. **Being very convincing with a shot fake allows you to buy that half second of time where the defender flinches (if they are a few yards from you) or where the defender dives in (if they are closer to you).** Either one allows you to dribble in the other direction, pass, or find room to shoot. Furthermore, your shot fake must look exactly like what? Your shot! Ensure that your arms, leg, and head all go up the same way when performing a shot fake or a shot.

Develop these BIG 3 skills to take your game to the next level. Say that you prefer the scissor over the jab step. That is fine, but make sure to practice it nonstop to ensure you are the best at the scissor. Do not waste time and effort trying to learn all the fancy skills that show up on SportsCenter highlights and in the Top 10 Plays. **In reality, practicing the complex moves decreases the amount of time spent on moves you know you can use successfully every game.** The "fancy" skills do not produce the same amount of results that the other, fundamental but very efficient skills do. Right now is an important time in your soccer career, so decide if you want to be a fancy player or if you want to be a player that scores a lot of goals. For the most part, they are not the same player.

Obviously, if you begin to excel with your BIG 3 skills and you are now able to dribble several defenders at once, like Lionel Messi, it will look fancy. **Therefore, now is the time to decide if you want to be the player that scores two goals a game and may have a few, if any, fancy goals over the course of a season or would you rather be that player that scores a few very spectacular goals a season because you want to use too much practice time on skills that are not efficient?** Choose wisely and choose now as you want to take the time to perfect the skills that you will use for years to come.

Chapter 5

Tier 2 – Scissor, Rolls, & Step Overs

We just discussed the Tier 1 skills that can be performed in the previous chapter. **Use the jab step when a defender is backpedaling, a self-pass when the defender is overcommitting and reaching in for the ball, and the shot fake when you are hoping to have the defender either flinch or lunge in the wrong direction.** Now let us take a look at the Tier 2 skills. The skills in this chapter are considered Tier 2 skills because they are not quite as important or useful as the Tier 1 skills, but can be a useful part of a soccer player's skill set.

The three moves that are considered Tier 2 soccer skills are the scissor, the roll, and the step over. For many players, when they are initially learning to do the scissor, they end up moving their leg and their foot over the ball. The motion they make is similar to that of a magician moving his wand over his hat during the magic trick of pulling a rabbit out of his hat. The "magic wand" motion is not good form and is not believable at all. Many people that teach a scissor tell the soccer player to reach their leg out for the ball, to go around the ball with their leg in a circular motion, and then push the ball away with the opposite foot. **The problem with this is if you are**

reaching forward for the ball to go around it with your foot, your hips never change direction, so the defender is not going to be faked out.

A good defender is going to be watching the ball just as much as they are watching your hips and if you are not showing that you plan to go one way with your body, they will not believe your scissor. Therefore, the trick when doing the scissor is to have your plant foot planted past the ball so that you just have to take a step past the ball with your other leg as it is rolling through your legs while you are dribbling the ball. **In a sense, a scissor is really just a jab step in front of the ball.** The reason that the scissor is a Tier 2 skill and the jab step is a Tier 1 skill is that even though they are used in the same situation when a defender is backpedaling, the scissor takes an extra step in order to step past the ball and that extra step takes extra time. As a result, a scissor is not as quick as a jab step and if you were only to practice one of these skills, it is highly recommended that it be the jab step.

There is a difference between a scissor and a double scissor. A scissor is when you only use one leg whereas a double scissor is when you use one leg to go around the ball and then you use the opposite leg as well to go around the ball, hence the "double" in a double scissor. **When doing a scissor, if you do a right-footed**

scissor, you are faking to the right, so you should be pushing the ball away with your left foot and pushing it towards the left. If you push it towards the right, you are faking in the direction that you are ultimately going, so you are telling the defender where you will go and then you will likely push it right into their shins.

Also, the reason that you should use the opposite foot to push the ball away is that it takes one less step. Using fewer steps will take less time and make you a quicker soccer player. If you perform a scissor with one foot and push it away with that same foot, it requires you to take three steps. The first step is the scissor, the second step with the opposite leg is to plant, and then the third step is to push the ball away with the same leg that did the scissor. Why add an extra step if it will only take extra time? If you do a right-footed scissor and you are faking to go to the right, then push it away with your left, which only takes two steps and then proceed to accelerate after your push.

The next Tier 2 move is the roll. The roll is to be performed with the bottom of your toes, but the problem with the roll is that you have to take your foot from the ground to the top of the ball, roll the ball, which crosses your feet, then uncross your feet, and take a touch forward with your opposite foot. Similarly to the self-pass, a roll is used when a defender is reaching in for the ball and you are just simply pushing the ball out of the way of their foot and then accelerating past the defender. **Because you are crossing your legs and taking the time to move your foot from the ground to the top of the ball, the roll is less athletic and more time-consuming than the self-pass, which is why it is a Tier 2 move.** However, the roll does provide a bit more control of the ball than the self-pass provides. Now, keep in mind that any time you do a roll or a self-pass, the ball should be going across the defender and then past them so the path the ball takes is the shape of an "L." Too often players will roll the ball diagonally, which only moves the ball closer to the defender's foot and makes it much easier for the defender to poke the ball away or to fully dispossess you.

The last skill of Tier 2 is the step over. **The step over is best used when your back is facing the direction that you need to go. Never use it when you are attacking forward at a defender that is backpedaling.** Many soccer players mistakenly call a scissor a step over, but they are different. With a scissor, the foot closest to the ball would be the one that goes around the ball. With the step over, as you are standing next to the ball, the leg farthest from the ball steps over the ball. Then, you bring your other leg around in order to plant your legs on the opposite side of the ball to push the ball away with the leg that initially started the step over. To perform the step over correctly, fully turn your shoulders in the direction you want the defender to believe that you are going in order to fake them in the wrong direction.

A step over is an excellent way to fake out a defender when they are on your back. **The step over makes them believe that you are going in one direction, but you intentionally miss the ball completely, so that you can push it out and accelerate with speed in the other direction.** The reason that this is also considered a Tier 2 move is because there are a lot fewer situations in a game that this skill will be needed when compared to the Tier 1 moves of a jab step, a self-pass, or a shot fake. However, this is a great move to have in your skill-set and is not similar to the other skills that we have discussed so far. Therefore, this move is one to practice.

In conclusion, a self-pass is going to be quicker than a roll, which is why a roll is a Tier 2 skill. Similarly, a scissor is going to be slower than a jab step. There are not as many opportunities in a game to use a step over, but it is still effective to do, so that you can dribble out of high-pressure situations with your back facing the direction of the field that you need to go in order to score.

Chapter 6

Tier 1 - Cuts & Shot Fakes

Now, we will be discussing the different types of shot fakes and cuts that you can use as a soccer player. First, a cut is a shot fake without actually faking the shot. **A cut is used to stop the ball from going one direction so you can quickly push the ball in another direction.** By pretending to kick the ball with any of the cuts that we are about to discuss, you will then turn that cut into a shot fake.

With a shot fake, it is critical to remember that a shot fake must look exactly like a shot. This means your arms must go up and your shooting leg must go up exactly the same way as a real shot when you perform a shot fake. If the form is not exactly the same, it might work the first and maybe even the second time, but after that, the defender will recognize the differences in your form and will not be faked out by your shot fakes anymore. Frequently, trainees' shot fakes are not believable because they are not raising their arms as big and they are not bringing their back leg as far back as if they were actually to shoot the ball. Therefore, make your shot and your shot fake look exactly the same so that you will more easily dribble past your opponent.

Shot Fakes		
Tier 1 Step On Step Out	Cut	Chop
Tier 2 Cruyff	V Pull Back	Jump Turn

The first shot fake that I often teach my trainees is the step on step out shot fake. A step on step out shot fake is simply pretending to shoot the ball, then stepping on it with the bottom of your foot instead of striking the ball. Then, with the same foot that stepped on the ball, take another step to plant to the side of the ball, so that your other leg can come through and push the ball in a different direction. **This step on step out is a great attacking shot fake because the entire time, your body and hips are still pointed in the direction you are looking to go up the field.** Whereas with many of the other shot fakes, you end up changing directions completely, so that if you were going forward and you performed a Cruyff on the ball, you would end up turning around and go in a backward direction. As we discussed in the previous chapter, when you stop the ball with the bottom of your foot, use the bottom of your toes to reach farther for the ball and to have the best feel for the ball once you make contact with it.

Another shot fake that is very useful is just cutting the ball with the inside of your foot. As the ball is moving on the field, pretend to shoot it but instead of striking it, just cut it with the inside of your foot so that it either stops, allowing you to push it quickly and accelerate away or cut it, so it starts to move in the opposite direction, so that you can also continue to accelerate away at speed. **A cut shot fake involves the ball staying in front of you, which is different from the Cruyff**, that we will be discussing in the next chapter. Because the ball is staying in front of you, this shot fake is better used when you have 2-3 yards between you and the defender.

If the defender is very close to you, then cutting the ball with the inside of your foot is not the best choice. The Cruyff is better to use because it will allow you to have the ball behind your body, which means you are between the defender and the ball to allow you to protect the ball more easily. With all shot fakes including a cut shot fake, it is beneficial to stop the ball because you know exactly where the ball will be and it makes it easier for you to push the ball away and accelerate after performing the cut shot fake. The disadvantage with the cut shot fake is that if the defender is too close to you, the defender will likely be able to reach the ball and take possession from you.

Therefore, the advantage of cutting the ball where it continues to move after changing direction is that you can cut it away from the defender's reach. However, the disadvantage of cutting the ball with it traveling in the direction you are about to go is that the ball will be further away from you. If you misjudge the defender's movement or do not see another defender on the opposing team, you will be less likely to protect the ball because it is now further away from your body.

Next, doing a shot fake where you cut the ball with the outside of your foot instead of the inside may also be referred to as a chop shot fake. **Performing a chop shot**

fake is excellent if you are looking to explode in the complete opposite direction you are currently going. When performing a chop shot fake, it is vital that when you reach for the ball, you have the outside of your foot entirely past the ball and planted on the ground, so that the ball is hitting the outside of your foot as it is rolling in order for it to stop. It is highly recommended that you stop the ball when performing a chop shot fake so that it is right next to your foot once you go to plant and push away in a different direction. The chop shot fake is a very explosive skill that buys you time in two ways. First, if your shot fake is performed well, the defender will try to block the shot or turn to avoid being hit with the shot. Second, you can explode away very quickly out of the chop shot fake. Cutting the ball with the outside of your foot places the ball exactly where you would want it when you go to dribble, which makes it a lot easier for you to accelerate away with speed.

Now, something to consider is that there is an advantage to performing a shot fake poorly if you are planning to do so. Specifically, doing a shot fake that you want the defender to realize is, in fact, a shot fake will often result in the defender lunging in or relaxing. Either one will allow you to take advantage of the situation. If the defender lunges in, this provides a great opportunity to push the ball away from their foot and accelerate past them, given their momentum is going in the opposite direction yours is going. If the defender relaxes for even half a second, this gives you an opportunity to take an actual shot, pass the ball to a teammate, or continue to dribble the defender.

In summary, we have discussed the three most efficient shot fakes that you can use. First, the step on step out is to be used when you are going up the field and want to continue to go up the field, but need to create space to dribble by a defender. Second, a cut shot fake allows you to keep the ball in front of you and will enable you to push the ball and accelerate away. This can be used to continue attacking forward or to go backward. Third, the chop shot fake is where you cut the ball with the outside of your foot and use this to explode in the opposite direction from which you came. Remember that all of these shot fakes are used in order to create space for your next move, pass, or shot.

Chapter 7

Tier 2 – Cuts & Shot Fakes

Similar to the foot skills discussed in earlier chapters that have 2 Tiers, so do the type of cuts used in the different shot fakes. Similarly to foot skills, there are certain shot fakes that are more efficient than others. The Tier 2 shot fakes are the Cruyff, the V pull back, and the jump turn.

Though a seemingly funny name, the Cruyff is named after the famous soccer player Johan Cruyff who played for the Netherlands National Team, as well as for clubs Ajax and Barcelona. Johan Cruyff made this cut famous. Therefore, the move was named after him. Recall from the previous chapter where it mentioned that the cut shot fake is where the ball is cut in front of your body.

The Cruyff is when you cut the ball, but leave yourself between the defender and the ball. In essence, you are cutting the ball behind your plant leg. After the Cruyff is performed, similar to all the other shot fakes, explode away by accelerating in the direction from which you came. The Cruyff is considered a Tier 2 move because you momentarily lose sight of the ball, which can make it difficult to know precisely where the ball is when you go to turn and accelerate away from pressure. As mentioned previously, the Cruyff is best used when the defender is very close to you, within 1-2 yards, and you want to have your body between you and the ball to better protect the ball from the defender. Like the chop shot fake, this skill is used to change your direction completely. Therefore, this is not a skill to use if you desire to continue an attack forward.

The next shot fake is the V pull back. Though this may sound a bit complicated, **this shot fake is when you fake your shot and then proceed to pull the ball backward using the bottom of the foot that pretended to shoot the ball. Then, use your other leg to push the ball and accelerate forward in the other direction, hence the "V" in the V pull back.** For example, if you did the shot fake with your left foot, as you were attacking to the left, you would pull the ball back with the bottom of your left foot and then push it with your right foot to attack towards the right. Like the step on step out shot fake or the cut shot fake, you can use this move to continue attacking forward. Since you are moving the ball as part of the shot fake, this is a useful skill when the defender is very close to you and has their legs reaching in for the ball.

The last shot fake to discuss is the jump turn shot fake. For the jump turn shot fake, instead of pulling the ball back with the bottom of your foot, as you would do in the V pull back, stop the ball with the bottom of your foot as you jump past the ball, landing with both feet at the same time on the other side of the ball. **Landing with both feet at the same time on the other side of the ball allows you to explode away in the direction from which you came.** Similar to the chop shot fake, this skill is beneficial to accelerate away from the defender.

In conclusion, focus primarily on the Tier 1 shot fakes. **Only work to develop the Tier 2 shot fakes once you have perfected the Tier 1 shot fakes.** The Tier 2 shot fakes (the Cruyff, the V pull back, and the jump turn) have their places when best to be used in a game, but more often than not, the Tier 1 shot fakes will be more efficient to use in most game situations. For any of these shot fakes, they can be used just as efficiently and effectively as pass fakes or cross fakes depending on the situation you find yourself in during a game. Therefore, do not only use these fakes when pretending to shoot but when pretending to pass and cross the ball too.

As it has been stated before, perfect practice makes perfect, so work on your form with these shot fakes and cuts. Remember that your shot fake must look exactly like your shot to ensure that the defender will either flinch and turn a little bit (buying you time) or that the defender will lunge out and try to stop your shot (allowing you to accelerate in a different direction to score, pass, or cross the ball). If the different Tiers and each of the skills within the Tiers seem like a lot to absorb at once, consider heading to UnderstandSoccer.com/free-printout in order to receive an outstanding summary that organizes and explains each of these skills in the different Tiers.

Chapter 8

Beating a Defender

To travel past a defender when dribbling, make sure that you aggressively push the ball and explode away after doing a foot skill. This chapter is an excerpt from the previous book in the Understand Soccer Series – *Soccer Shooting & Finishing: A Step-by-Step Guide on How to Score.* **The four essential reasons for an aggressive push are:**

1. **It provides space between you and the defender.** Therefore, you will have slightly more time to pick your head up to see where the goalie is and where to aim your shot.

2. If you accelerate after pushing the ball, you will have more speed running to the ball. **If you have more speed running to the ball, you are naturally going to have a more powerful shot.** For example, imagine you are standing still and you strike a shot with your foot planted next to the ball versus having a good three to four step run up on the ball. You will kick it a lot further with a running start when your momentum, your body, and your hips can travel through the ball when you strike your shot.

3. An aggressive push past the defender gets you closer to the net. **The closer you are to the net, the more accurate you will be as the net becomes bigger.** Additionally, being closer to the net, the goalie is going to have less time to react to stop your shot.

4. **When you explosively push the ball closer to the net, the goalkeeper will have less time to react to your shot.** If the goalie has less time to react to your shot, the greater the chance that your shot will go in. Now, keep in mind that pushing the ball too far will give the ball to the opponent's goalkeeper.

       Pushing the ball past a defender is best suited for when you have just performed a foot skill. You push the ball with the outside portion of your laces about

5-7 yards behind the defender. Please keep in mind faster players can afford to push the ball further than slower players. Also, a 5-7 yard push works great when you are going against only one defender, but if there is another defender behind the defender you are approaching, you would want to first use a foot skill. Then, you would use a smaller push of the ball that will only go 2-3 yards. This will help you avoid pushing the ball into the supporting defender's feet.

It is critical that you go into a game with the mindset that you will beat defenders that will allow you to take shots. If your current mindset has you a little bit scared to go against a defender 1v1, you are likely not going to be successful. You have to have confidence in yourself, so as you read this book and implement the tips, tricks, tweaks, and techniques this book mentions, you will gain confidence in your ability to beat a defender and strike a quality shot on net.

Consider the fact that a defender is typically running backward when you are going against them. **Therefore, it is crucial to understand that a defender running backward will not be as quick as an attacker running forward.** As a result, an attacker's speed is critical because the higher the pace the forward attacks with, the harder it will be for the defender to keep up while staying balanced. Additionally, when you explode past a defender, there is a brief moment when the defender is transitioning from running backward to turning their body to run forward to keep up with you. If your initial push is explosive enough, the defender will not have time to transition their body's momentum from running backward to running forward quickly enough to stop you. Watch Eden Hazard, the Chelsea and Belgium National team member to see a player that can effectively take first touches and push the ball efficiently past defenders, seemingly with ease.

Furthermore, you do not have to be entirely past the defender to take a shot. All you need is just a little bit of space to create a shot that is effective and on target. If the defender has been covering you well during the game, shooting into their shins/ankles is not going to help your team at all, but keep in mind that you miss 100% of the shots you do not take. It is much more important for a soccer team to try to increase the volume of its shots because more shots result in more chances for the ball to go in.

Let us play out a situation; a team that takes 30 shots in a game compared to a team that takes five really good shots. The team that takes 30 shots is still probably going to win because there are more opportunities for the goalie to accidentally make a mistake, for the shooting team to have a lucky shot, or for the goalie to give up a rebound resulting in a teammate shooting the ball into the back of the net.

Chapter 9

Dribbling with Both Feet

As a soccer player, your primary objective is to beat the other team in the game. Therefore, if the goal is to win, you should be willing to do what it takes to place yourself in better situations in order to succeed.

As a result, it is important that you are able to use both of your feet. Just because you have two feet, I am not suggesting that you have to be able to dribble with both of them equally. **However, both feet should be able to do the skill needed to dribble by the defender, to pass the ball, to cross the ball, or to take a shot on net.** Using both feet allows you to become more elusive and unpredictable.

Anytime you are performing a drill, weaving in and out of cones at practice, or going up against the defender, you can successfully dribble through or past the obstacle with both feet. **Having a few mastered moves in situations where you are forced to use your opposite foot will be enough for the defender to have to respect it.** It is recommended that you perform the drill in one direction and then switch up the direction of the cones so if you were using right-footed jab steps, now you will be using a left-footed jab step. If you were using right-footed cut shot fakes, now you can use left-footed cut shot fakes and right to left self-passes become left to right self-passes. Being able to dribble with both feet gives you more options for where you can go with the ball and how you can dribble around a defender. As mentioned in the book *Soccer Shooting and Finishing: A Step-by-Step Guide on How to Score*, it is very important that you can shoot with both feet and related to this book, it is just as important that you can dribble with both feet.

Whatever space the defender is giving you, you need to be able to use it efficiently. If the defender is defending you well, you will still be able to create space with your foot skills and abilities. **Countless players that I have played with and have trained are only good with one foot, usually their right foot and this makes them incredibly predictable and easy to stop.** All a defender needs to do is reduce their ability to attack to their right. If they cannot go to their right side, they cannot use their right foot to shoot and you have made them an ineffective soccer player. On the other hand, a good defender will notice if you are only good with one foot and make sure that you cannot use your dominant foot as effectively as you would hope to in a game.

Let us play out an example. **If you only dribble with your right foot, right-footed skills will often move the ball to your left foot, making it easier to shoot with your left foot.** As a result, if you cannot dribble with your left foot, you will often find it difficult to move the ball to the right side of your body, so that you can use your right foot to shoot. The opposite applies for left-footed soccer players.

Furthermore, just as much as being able to practice with it and develop it is essential, but having a quality mindset about your opposite foot is just as important too. **Also, notice that in this entire chapter, it was never called it a "weak foot," only your "opposite foot."** Often, a person will believe their opposite foot is weak and there is little they can do to improve it simply because they call their opposite foot their "weak foot." This limiting belief makes it so a player does not take steps to improve their abilities to use their opposite foot. It is highly recommended that you always call it your opposite foot so that you do not associate that negative meaning with "weak" in your mind and ultimately into your game.

Look at the great soccer players of all time, it is difficult to find a handful of the greatest that could only use one foot because the greatest soccer players know that being able to go in either direction or use either foot will allow them to increase the probability of success on the field and furthering their playing career. Since you are a player, parent, or coach reading this book, you would not be spending the time learning this information if you did not care about improving. Therefore, one of the quickest things that you can do to grow and to advance your game on the field is to focus on developing your opposite foot so you can use either foot when you are dribbling the ball up the field and past the opposing team.

Chapter 10

Do Not Be Selfish

In soccer, it is essential that your teammates do not consider you as a selfish soccer player. Given that you are learning from the steps in this book to improve your ability to dribble the ball, you will be more likely to want to dribble past players instead of immediately looking for an open pass. **As a result, if you start to consistently dribble instead of pass as you are developing your foot skills, many of your teammates might begin to view you as being selfish.** To clarify, if being selfish in specific instances will allow you to score, which will further your team's objective, then you can make the argument that this selfishness is needed and helpful to win.

However, when you have a blatantly obvious opportunity to pass the ball to your teammate that will make it easier for them to score than you, and you decide that it is better for you to keep dribbling, these are the situations that you should avoid. These situations result in teammates thinking that you are in it for yourself, which diminishes the trust they have with you. **Always keep in the back of your mind that your team's principal objective is to win the game.** Therefore, if a pass will better serve your team, pass the ball. If dribbling the ball will better help your team, then dribble the ball. The situation determines if you will be called selfish by your teammates. If you are a forward attacking towards the opposition's net and there are no teammates lateral with you or in front of you to pass the ball, then in these situations, it is entirely appropriate for you to take on a defender by using your foot skills to create space to fire off a shot. Another case that it is acceptable to dribble is when a poor pass has been played to you and the defender is practically on top of you. Use your foot skills to escape this uncertain situation as it is more difficult to pick your head up to find someone to pass to when the other team's player is smothering you.

You may be wondering if there is ever a situation where it is acceptable to be blatantly selfish. **As a general rule of thumb in soccer, you do not want to be selfish. However, if you observe the most celebrated soccer players that have ever graced the pitch, you will notice that there is a bit of selfishness to their character and in their play.** They knew to develop as a soccer player, they needed the ball at their feet. In order to score, they need the ball at their feet. To be recognized by scouts, coaches, parents, and other players, they understood that they need the ball at their feet. You may consider this as a player that is merely taking responsibility for their team, but understand that many others will see it as you are placing your own interests before the team's interests.

Therefore, depending on where you are in your career and depending if there are scouts or potential coaches at a game, it can understandably sway you to be a bit more selfish to show off your abilities. Luckily, there is an easy workaround for this. **Make sure you are always demanding and yelling for the ball because if you possess the ball more often, you will have more opportunities to show your skills off.**

Also, you will have more opportunities to pass the ball, so that the coaches and scouts can see your abilities with the ball and passing abilities. **Furthermore, when you are not in an actual competitive game, such as when you are playing in practice, playing pickup soccer, or with a bunch of your friends while working on your soccer skills, it is more appropriate to be a bit more selfish.** Again, the underlying belief is that to become better at soccer, you need the ball at your feet. Recall the pyramid at the beginning of this book and consider diving into one of the soccer specific sections. Pick a few of the skills in that area to work on and emphasize them when you are practicing.

Obviously, this is not true for all things. While reading this book, a soccer ball is probably not at your feet and you are still becoming better at soccer by increasing your knowledge of how to play the game. In general, however, the reason certain countries can produce top soccer talent is that they ensure their youth players have many opportunities for significantly more touches on the ball. 3v3 and 5v5 games result in foreign players being more confident in game situations.

It does take a bit of experience to find the happy medium between passing the ball, dribbling to beat a defender, and shooting to score. **Do not be the player that expects to win the game for your team each time you touch the ball.** It will be detrimental for your team if every time you obtain the ball, you have to dribble it before you make a pass. Remember, there are plenty of opportunities to win the game for your team, but make sure you are taking the necessary steps and making the appropriate passes to place your team in high-quality situations. Use your growing dribbling and foot skills when necessary to accomplish your team's goal of winning.

In conclusion, possess the ball more to have more opportunities to dribble and pass. When you are caught in tight situations or you are the person with the ball attacking the defender with no options to pass laterally or up the field, then dribble in this situation. It is important to consider the teammates that you are playing with. **If you are the least talented one on the field then it is more appropriate for you to pass more. If you are the most talented player on the field, it is appropriate for you to dribble a bit more** when necessary to give your team a quality chance at scoring. Furthermore, use practice time, pick-up games, and scrimmages to be a bit more selfish, knowing that more touches on the ball and learning from mistakes that you have made will increase your abilities when game time comes around.

Chapter 11

1v1s

A soccer player that can go up against one defender and win at least 80% of the time is very rare in soccer. These players are coveted by coaches because they know that this player will be able to create space away from the opposition to take more shots on net. **More shots generally means a much higher probability for goals or rebounds that turn into goals.** Please understand that you still want to make good decisions and avoid dribbling just to take unreasonable shots. Therefore, as a soccer player developing your skills to perform in 1v1 situations successfully, **consider the following three things:**

1. Use a foot skill.
2. Attack with speed.
3. Aim to use your dominant foot to shoot.

First, use a foot skill!!! Using a foot skill to create space is one piece of advice that should most definitely be followed in a 1v1 situation, but sadly few players actually do. Most wait to pass the ball to a supporting teammate or try to outrun the opposition by kicking the ball past the defender and using his or her speed. Specifically, use a jab step or a scissor to fake as if you are going to your opposite foot. Done correctly, this will enable you to have created a foot or two of space to explode forward with your dominant foot. An attacking skill where the defender is backpedaling often lures the defender to commit to going in the wrong direction. If the defender goes the wrong way, he or she will be off balance, which significantly increases the chance for you to take your shot without it being blocked or even for you to dribble entirely past the defender, allowing you a one-on-one opportunity with the opponent's goalie.

Next, attack with speed. A 1v1 situation is excellent for a forward that usually has two or three defenders covering them. Attack as if you do not have any support coming, but do not be afraid to make a pass if you see a teammate out of the corner of your eye. Do not look straight down at the ball when dribbling. Instead, look five or so yards past the ball to see a teammate or potentially another defender. In addition, occasionally take a quick glance to see where the goalkeeper is because, in 1v1 situations, goalies will often come further out of their net, which may present you an excellent opportunity to chip the ball over them.

Goalies will often creep up the field and out of their net. They realize that a forward is trained to dribble past a defender and has a pretty good chance of winning the 1v1 battle against the defender. This frees the attacker to have a shot or dribble towards the net, so the goalie will want to come out a little bit to cut down the angle of the shot. If the goalkeeper is standing square in the middle of the net when the striker shoots, there is very little chance that they will save shots that are close to either of the posts. However, if the goalie comes out and cuts the angle off, they are limiting the amount of net into which the striker can shoot. **The speed after the skill is critical to create the space and separation between you and the defender.** Jog by the defender and they will sprint to catch up. Sprint by the defender and you will most likely not have to beat them again on that specific attempt to score.

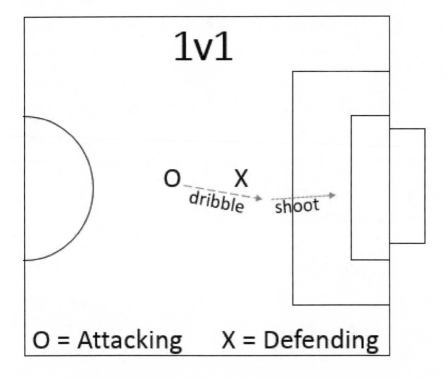

Lastly, whenever you have a 1v1 situation while attacking towards the other team's net, your goal should be to take your shot with your dominant foot. Obviously, the foot that you are more comfortable using will provide a more accurate and powerful shot on target compared to your opposite foot. **In a 1v1, because only one person is defending you, a good striker will go in the direction that he or she wants, as shown in the image, when the defender is directly in front of them.** Therefore, if you are right-footed, practice those left-footed jab steps and scissor to ensure that the ball ends up on your right foot when you go to shoot.

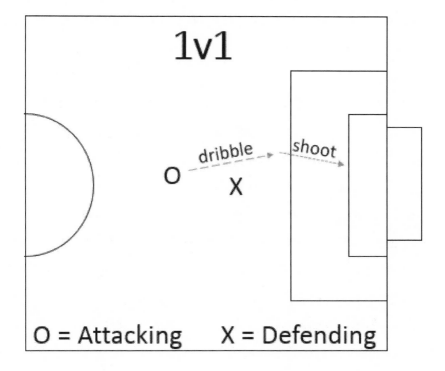

However, you do not want to go to your dominant foot 100% of the time because, on occasion, the defender will be letting you go to your opposite foot by completely cutting off your path up the field towards your dominant foot, as shown in this image. **In a situation where the**

defender gives you a lot of space to your opposite foot, take it because you will be able to push well past the defender to ensure that you can take a shot with your opposite foot. Since you will have much more space than going to your dominant foot, it will be easier for you to take a powerful and well-driven shot on target when you go to strike the ball. Otherwise, use a jab step, scissor, or inside of the foot shot fake to help create space to enable you to travel to your dominant foot. Also, consider if you have gone against that defender already in the game. Use the information on what makes your opponent uncomfortable, what worked, and what you think may work to increase your chance of beating them.

To conclude, your objectives when attacking in a 1v1 are to use a skill to create space, attack with speed to take the space that the foot skill created, and more often than not, use a foot skill that will move the ball to your dominant foot when you go to strike the ball. Capitalize on 1v1s to ensure you score a goal for your team and build your confidence as a soccer player. This chapter may also be found in the previous book in the Understand Soccer Series – *Soccer Shooting & Finishing: A Step-by-Step Guide on How to Score*. 1v1s are related to dribbling and foot skills as much as they are related to shooting and finishing. If you found this chapter helpful, pick up the *Soccer Shooting & Finishing* Book for chapters on 2v1s, 1v2s, and 2v2s, among other topics.

Chapter 12

Turning with a Defender on Your Backside

As a soccer player that is looking to score, you will often find yourself with your back turned towards the very thing you are aiming to score in, the other team's net. **It is incredibly important that you are able to effectively receive a pass, turn your body, and explode up the field.** Ideally, you should be able to do this all in one motion. Recently, this topic was the main focus of a training session for one of my trainees, Kylie Kade, who has aspirations of playing for the United States Women's National Team. **Therefore, steps to consider when turning with a defender on your backside are:**

1. Look over your shoulder before you receive the pass to feel comfortable demanding the ball if you have space and believe you can do something productive for your team. **(Have your head on a swivel.)**

2. **Use your arm** to help you balance and prevent the opposing team's defender from going around you to cut off the pass.

3. Either have your shoulders pointed directly at the ball when it is coming towards you (so that you are not showing which way you are going) or **be tricky by using**

your body to fake like you are going one way when you are planning to push the ball in the other direction.

4. Use the outside of your foot to push the ball. **It is not a first touch you are looking to take but a first step that includes the first touch**, so that you can accelerate away more quickly from the defender.

First, it cannot be stressed enough that you should look behind your shoulder when you are preparing to receive a pass. Depending on the situation, it may be best to just hold the ball and wait for support. A quick look will allow you to know where you should push the ball or even if you should request a pass at all from a teammate. Do not twist at the hips to look behind you because this takes too much time. **Only turn your head by using your neck to make sure that you can take a swift look at the field and the players behind you.** If you do this and determine that you have space to attack then yell for the ball and demand that it be passed to you.

Second, you will very rarely be called for having your hands on an opponent. As such, when you are ready to receive the pass with your back facing the net you are looking to score in, keep your arm up for balance, but especially to hold back the defender to ensure you are the one to receive the pass and not the other team. Having your arm up does not mean that you should hold onto them, but should place your forearm against them to slow their attempt to travel around you to intercept the ball. Also, having your arm up allows you to feel if the defender is more towards either side of you, which would factor into your decision on how to turn.

Third, never show the defender where you are going by revealing it to him or her with your body. When turning with your back to the goal and a defender is on your backside, either have your shoulders pointed directly at the ball when it is coming towards you or be deceptive and use your body to fake as if you are going one way when you are planning to push the ball in the other direction. Having your body pointed directly at the ball does not reveal to the defender which way you are going, which is good, but the defender will only commit to going in a direction that they believe you will be pushing the ball. This is why it is so effective to use your body to pretend as if you are going one way, while your real intentions are to go the other way.

Therefore, have your shoulders turned slightly in the direction that you want your defender to think you are going. **Many defenders read the opposing player's body language as much as they read where the ball is currently located when judging how to stop a player attacking with the ball.** Therefore, if you show the defender the direction that you are not going, they will often overcommit to the wrong side. If the defender commits to the wrong side, it will make it very easy for you to beat the defender without worrying about slowing the speed of play or having the defender steal the ball.

When taking a deceptive first touch, there are two options. First, if you are looking to take your first touch in the space to the area behind you to the right, then turn your body/shoulders slightly to left (so the defender will assume you are going to the left) and raise your right leg so it looks like you will be pushing to the left.

However, at the last second, before receiving the pass, move your right leg across your body so that you can push with the outside of your foot to go to the space behind you to the right. Do the opposite of this if you looking to go to the space behind you on the field, to the left. The second option for when you want to deceive a defender into thinking you are going to the area to the left behind you, when you are really looking to go to the right is start by pointing your body/shoulders slightly to the left, then look like you are going to push the ball with your left foot.

However, pretend to push the ball with your left foot a bit too early, so that you can plant that left leg on the ground, and raise your right leg across your body to push the ball with the outside of your right foot. Think of this as a jab/feint where you miss receiving the ball with your left foot and take it with your right. You can choose which move suits you better. The first option takes some flexible ankles and the ability to pivot with the plant foot that is already on the ground. The second option provides for a very stable plant of the left foot just after you have purposely missed the ball to allow for quick acceleration out with your right foot. Therefore, the second option is the preferred option, but please try both and see which one is more fluid for you.

Fourth, it is ideal to use the outside of your foot to push the ball when turning into the space diagonally behind you because it allows you to take your first touch/step without having your legs crossed when you plant to explode away. Crossing your legs is very unathletic and should be avoided when possible as it is hard to explode with speed and it is easier to become unbalanced. It is especially important to be active and on the toes/balls of your feet to be ready for any pass.

To take a smaller touch when turning with a defender on your backside, take your first touch/step with the outside of your foot toward your toes because this is a softer area on your foot and the ball will not bounce off as powerfully. For a bigger touch, use the portion of your outside foot towards your heels to push the ball since the ball will be pushed with the harder area of the outside of your foot. **Push the ball far enough to create space between you and the defender.**

Combine these four steps to become a deceptive forward that is quickly able to make progress up the field, even if their back is turned to it. Turning with your back towards the net you need to score on is a skill that most soccer players never learn. However, if this skill is mastered, it will place you in an elite class of forwards that are confident and able to control the ball. Several players to watch for good examples and that are known for their ability to be a point man (a big presence capable of winning balls out of the air and connecting passes for smaller/quicker players) are Karim Benzema, Edinson Cavani, Gonzalo Higuaín, Olivier Giroud, and Zlatan Ibrahimović.

Chapter 13

The Nutmeg

I want to start out this chapter by saying though it feels like you dominated another player when you complete a nutmeg on an opponent, it is much more likely to be an unsuccessful attempt at pushing the ball between their legs. As mentioned in previous chapters and in previous books, we want to do the things that will give us the highest probability of success. This is why more efficient moves are found in Tier 1 and less efficient moves are located in Tier 2. **Therefore, nutmegs often result in turnovers, so they are not the best thing to pursue even though many players make them out to be very important.**

Your ultimate goal is to shoot that ball into the back of the net more times than the other team does and by aiming to do a nutmeg, it will decrease your chances of being successful. As a result, avoid spending too much practice time working on going through other players, but instead focus on the ways to shoot, dribble, and pass around other players. **Think about it; you have to push the ball through the defender's legs and travel entirely to the other side of them to maintain possession of the ball.** This is the opposite of what was discussed in the

1v1s chapter of creating just enough space to take a shot. Because you have to go through the defender, your likelihood of pulling it off is significantly reduced. Let us not forget that a defender going for a nutmeg can lead to an easy goal by the other team.

Oftentimes, when you go for a nutmeg, you push the ball into the oncoming players' shins and their momentum is carrying them past you with the ball that you just gave them. They do not even need to dribble by you now because you were trying to travel to the other side of them after you hoped to push the ball between their legs. Furthermore, even if you dribble the ball through their legs, there is a high chance they will stick their arms out and block you from traveling to the other side of them. **If you do not maintain possession after pushing the ball through their legs, the nutmeg does not count!**

If you are still interested in a skill that works for me to do a nutmeg, which was taught to me by my mentor Aaron Byrd, then use a slightly modified V pull back. If the ball is outside your left shoulder, instead of using your left foot to pull the ball back, use your right foot to start pulling it back. Beginning the V pull back with the opposite foot that is closest to the defender will prompt the defender to try to place their foot in the lane that you would pull the ball in if you were going to do the V pull back. At the last second, pull the ball back only slightly then proceed to push it between the defender's open legs. This skill has allowed me to nutmeg (meg) many opposing players and many trainees. Going for nutmegs is something that I might do once in an entire season.

I have a friend that is the king of the "meg," Youssef Hodroj. On the one hand, his recommendation is similar to mine in that he also recommends rarely going for a nutmeg in a game because it is too risky. On the other hand, he believes that a nutmeg is an important concept to the art of humiliating your opponent and getting into their head. **In reality, if you are able to complete a nutmeg on an opposing player, then there is a high chance that he or she will keep their legs closer together, which will make it easier for you to push by them later in the game.**

Furthermore, Youssef is quick to point out that soccer is a very situational game and depends heavily on your positioning relative to the defender. It is best to understand that skills that you use force them to plant heavily on one foot, which will cause them to reach for the ball with their other foot. This reach provides a large space between their feet increasing the chance you can push the ball through their legs and maintain possession of it on the other side of them.

In short, use the nutmeg very rarely. When you are with friends or playing in a pick-up game, this is an optimal time to work on the skill that will allow you to do a nutmeg on your opponent. The Nutmeg does not fall into Tier 1 or Tier 2 of the skills mentioned in this book because it is a move that often does not work. In fact, you often end up pushing the ball into the defender's shins as his or her momentum is carrying them towards your net with little chance of you being able to slow them down because your momentum is taking you in the opposite direction.

Chapter 14

Why Most Skills Are Unnecessary

As you have been reading, you may have noticed that there are several skills that you have probably heard of are not included in the contents of this book. This is for a good reason because **many skills are distracting at best for a soccer player.** In life, you can easily have too many things going on. The more things you have on your plate, the less you can focus on each one of the items individually. Focusing on too many things in soccer is no different. If you start spending considerable practice time on skills that are not very useful in a game, this will take away practice time from the important skills that you will need in every single game. Ultimately, spreading yourself too thin will result in you being a "jack of all trades (skills) but a master of none." In soccer, if you can master the Tier 1 foot skills, the Tier 1 shot fakes and potentially the step over, you will have all the necessary tools to dribble your way through the other team.

Though the Rainbow, Akocha, Elastico/Snake, Roll to Heel, Hocus Pocus, Ronaldo Chop, Rivelino... are exciting foot skills to learn and to help develop your touch, they are not needed. And yes, for those of you who have never heard of these before, these are all names of skills that you can perform, among many others. If you are curious about any of them, feel free to search for them on YouTube, but only to know what they are, but not to practice them. Consider practicing them only if you can perform the jab step, the self-pass, and the three types of shot fakes 10 times each, without making a single mistake. Even then, you would be better off mastering the Tier 2 skills, perfecting your ability to shoot, developing your ability to pass and receive, and learning how to dispossess the other team of the ball efficiently.

To sum up, most skills that you may see or hear about are unnecessary and only worth practicing if you have perfected the skills in the different Tiers mentioned in this book and the other topics covered in separate books as shown on the Individual Soccer Player's Pyramid. Similarly to how playing the Crossbar Challenge or working on Bicycle Kicks can be detrimental, as discussed in the book Soccer Shooting & Finishing, the Rainbow, Akocha, Elastico/Snake, Roll to Heel, Hocus Pocus, Ronaldo Chop, Rivelino,... can hinder you too. There is a concept in Economics called "opportunity cost" that is perfect to understand in this situation.

Specifically, opportunity cost is the cost of not doing certain things because you chose to do something else. The cost of the fancy skills mentioned previously is too high because you have to give up practice time on what is most important. Be protective of your practice time and emphasize the abilities that are most commonly used in a game to ensure that you become an all-star soccer player as quickly as possible.

Chapter 15

The Field/Terrain Matters

Considering that the goal of dribbling is to help your team score, **the field on which you are playing and the weather conditions you are playing in make a big difference.** Whether it is 75°F and sunny or 35°F with freezing cold rain, these factors have a massive impact on whether you should dribble a lot or only a little in a game.

Most games, practices, and scrimmages will be played in relatively nice weather. The soccer season's timeline is often spaced out to where you are avoiding those cold weather months. **Therefore, most of your touches on the ball tend to be when the weather conditions are good or you are inside of a building, where the weather conditions are consistent and do not have an impact on the game whatsoever.** Due to the fact that most of your practice time is done in relatively comfortable temperatures and probably on well-groomed fields, if you find yourself playing in a game where the field is rough, the grass is too long, or the weather conditions are sub-optimal, this is a situation where you want to reduce the number of foot skills used during the game. Since so many of your touches are done in a weather controlled environment or on a perfectly groomed field, your touch will be off in a game where the ball is wet or the field is bumpy.

Poor fields or weather conditions cause your dribbling abilities to be lessened and increase the chance that the opposing team will be able to steal the ball as you attempt your foot skills in the game. Therefore, you will not want to rely heavily on your foot skills and dribbling skills in a poor weather condition game. **You can use these type of games to your advantage by understanding that simple passes will often be better.** When it is raining outside, take more shots on net knowing the ball may skip causing the goalie to misjudge the ball. Similarly, the goalie will be able to block shots but give up many rebounds because the ball is slippery, making it easy for your team to convert those rebounds into goals.

A good example involves professional soccer clubs across Europe. When a home team is playing an opponent that has excellent foot skills, the stadium managers will have their soccer field watered just before game time. Pre-game field watering causes for a ball that is more difficult to dribble, which will reduce the opponent's foot skill and dribbling abilities.

Similarly, if it is 95°F out and there is a blazing sun, this is also an extreme playing condition that requires smarts on your part. Specifically, you will lose energy more quickly and **few things deplete your energy reserves as much as trying to use your foot skills to dribble around several defenders on the other team**. Think about it, with all of the accelerating required after many of the foot skills, this explosive push and acceleration will tire you. In 95°F weather, it will tire you 2-3 times as fast. Therefore, hot games are great opportunities to let the ball do the work, by creating space with your passing and receiving abilities. Check out the fourth book in the Understand Soccer Series, *Soccer Passing & Receiving: How to Work with Your Teammates*, to learn the tips and tricks to take your passing and receiving to the next level.

Now, considering that you will have times where you are playing in poor weather conditions, **it does help to practice in those conditions**. You will be more comfortable with the ball at your feet and using foot skills on a bumpy field, during a rainstorm, through high winds, or on days where the temperature is high. Knowing you have practiced in these conditions will give you the confidence and the experience to make you a better-rounded player. A good soccer player will recognize how the weather will impact their game and adjust their playing style accordingly.

Chapter 16

How to Practice Dribbling and Fast Footwork

With all things, <u>perfect</u> practice makes perfect. When it comes to soccer, it is no different. Practicing to be a good dribbler with the proper form will surely make you a better dribbler. Therefore, the following is a fast footwork warm-up that I will often have my trainees perform when I am first working with them to see how good their technical abilities are. Also, the fast footwork acts as an excellent warm-up for 10 or so minutes in the first portion of practice. **This warm-up increases the number of touches that a player gets on the ball.** Set up a cone on the field that is about 15 to 20 yards away from another cone on the field so that the fast footwork is practiced in between the cones as follows:

1. Small Dribbles
2. Speed Dribbles
3. Outs and Ins
4. Push Stop
5. Self-Passes
6. Roll Touch
7. Rolls
8. Roll Stop
9. Step On Step Outs
10. Touch Scissor

1. **Small Dribbles** - With your toes pointed down and in, push the ball forward with the bone of your foot. Go for as many touches as possible from one cone to the other. Then, switch feet and repeat.

2. **Speed Dribbles** - With your toes pointed down and in, push the ball forward with the bone of your foot. Go for a touch every single step from one cone to the other. Then, switch feet and repeat.

3. **Out and Ins** - With your toes pointed down and in, push the ball diagonal with the bone of your foot (out) and then cut the ball with the inside of your foot (in). Go for as many touches as possible from one cone to the other. Then, switch feet and repeat.

4. **Push Stop** - With your toes pointed down and in, push the ball forward with the bone of your foot then stop the ball with the bottom of the same foot that pushed the ball, then immediately switch feet and repeat.

5. **Self-Passes** - using both feet, perform a pass from one foot to the next. The foot that receives the pass pushes the ball forward with the inside of the foot. Then using the same foot that pushed it, your next touch passes the ball back across your body so you can push the ball forward with the other foot.

6. **Roll Touch** - Facing forward, roll the ball across your body, then take a touch up with the opposite foot. Then with the opposite foot, roll the ball back across your body and push the ball up with the foot that did not roll the ball.

7. **Rolls** - With your body turned to the right and the side of your shoulder pointed towards the opposite cone, roll the ball using the bottom of your foot. Repeat with the opposite foot. When rolling the ball with the bottom of your foot, always use the bottom of your toes. Using the bottom of your heel or the bottom of the middle of your foot will not allow you to reach as far, your foot is more likely to bounce off the ball, and you have the most nerve endings in your foot in your toes. Having the most nerve endings in your toes means your toes have the best feel for the ball.

8. **Roll Stop** - Similarly with your shoulders turned sideways, roll the ball with the bottom of your toes, but stop the ball with the inside of your opposite foot. Then, with the same foot that rolled the ball, roll the ball again. Repeat this with the left foot.

9. **Step On Step Outs** - With your toes pointed down and in, push the ball diagonal with the bone of your foot. Then, with the same foot that pushed the ball, stop it with the bottom of your toes. Then, immediately push the ball diagonal with your other foot and stop it with the bottom of

the same foot that pushed the ball. Then repeat going back and forth using both feet.

10. **Touch Scissor** - Using only one foot, touch the ball forward with your toes pointed down and in. Then, with the same foot do a scissor. Then, move the ball with the same foot and do another scissor.

Note: Set up a line of cones with each cone spaced one yard apart. Perform these fast footwork skills between cones to increase your precision and accuracy of your touch.

One thing that is so exciting about this warm-up is that it does warm up a player significantly. A soccer player is moving a lot and taking many touches. In fact, in the book *The Compound Effect*, research was done on why Brazil can consistently turn out great soccer players at a higher rate than other countries. What was found was as children are growing up in Brazil, they grow up playing in games that have much smaller numbers. They are much more likely to play in a 4v4 or 5v5 in their leagues and competitions. The low number of players in each game is the opposite of what American children have become accustomed to, who at a relatively young age, are already playing in 11v11 games. You are likely already seeing the problem with this. **The more people on the field means**

the fewer touches any of the soccer players will have on the ball.

To become better with the ball, you need to take more touches and the Brazilian kids on average are taking two to three touches in a game for every one touch an American child obtains. Whether these are futsal or beach soccer games, both styles are 5-a-side and emphasize good ball control, agility, and a touch of finesse. As a result, it is no surprise that they are often much more skilled and better on the ball than the American youth players. **That is why the fast footwork above is so important because it allows yourself and your players to have a ton more touches on the ball that you or your team would not have had the opportunity to have otherwise.**

More touches on the ball will increase a soccer player's confidence with the ball. This increased confidence with the ball makes it more likely for them to want to actually dribble and develop their foot skills. Whereas, players that are lacking confidence, try to kick the ball away as soon as they receive it, so they hopefully can trick the other people into thinking that they are good soccer players, when in reality, they are really struggling and lacking the self-esteem that would allow them to improve.

In conclusion, use the fast footwork previously discussed before a game, during a practice, or even in your basement or backyard to increase the number of touches that you will be taking every single week. **Every additional touch you take is an additional opportunity to become better and grow at a faster rate than the other players you play with and against.** Understanding this concept is exciting because just by slightly modifying the way that you practice, you can ensure that your practice time is much better spent than your competition.

Chapter 17

Easy Drills With or Without Cones

This next chapter has easy drills to perform that allow you to practice your foot skills. The first section is a recommendation if you do not have cones. The second section is a course to set up if you do have cones.

Without Cones:

- Use two lines on the field that are 5 yards apart or the 6-yard box.
- Starting at one of the lines, push the ball with your toe down and in using the bone of your foot to the other line. (Only take one touch to travel to the other line.)
- Once at the other line, perform a shot fake. (Make sure it looks the same as your shot.)
- Then, accelerate back to the line where you started. (Only take one touch to travel back to the starting line.)
- Next, perform another shot fake. (Alternate between right and left footed shot fakes.)

Perform a set of 10 shot fakes (5 right footed and 5 left footed) starting with the cut shot fake. Perform 6 sets total. Switch the shot fake you use each time.

My recommendation is to do the Tier 1 shot fakes; cut, chop, and step on step out two times each. However, you may grow bored of doing the same skill more than once. If so, then perform the Tier 2 shot fakes (jump turn, Cruyff, and V pull back) too. Generally, this is advised against because it is better to be perfect at a few skills in soccer than to be okay at many skills.

With 9-10 Cones:
- Perform the drill as pictured below:

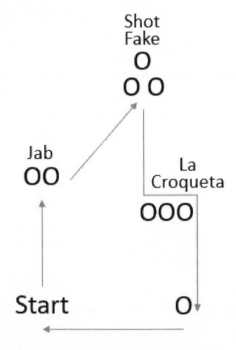

- Have each of the skills roughly 5 yards apart.
- Attack the first two cones "OO" and perform a left-footed jab step.
- Accelerate to the shot fake (The three "Os" in a triangle).

- Perform a right-footed chop shot fake.
- Accelerate with one push from your right foot to the "OOO" la croqueta.
- Do a la croqueta/self-pass by passing the ball from your right foot to your left foot.
- Accelerate to the "O" and use a right-footed chop just past the cone.
- Finally, accelerate back to the start.

Notes: Use only one push to accelerate to the next set of cones. Dribble with your head slightly up, not straight down at the ball. Make your shot fake look believable. This drill can be easily reversed to work on your skills in the opposite direction.

Conclusion

The main thing is to keep the main thing the main thing. **In soccer, the main thing to keep in mind is to develop the abilities that you are most likely to use on the field, without spending too much time on things that would be used only occasionally.** Referring back to the preface of this book, the Individual's Pyramid of Importance concept is an excellent indicator for all of the topics in soccer to emphasize how your practice time should be spent. For this book specifically, keep in mind that most of your time should be spent on the Tier 1 skills. If you master them, then maybe spend a bit of time on the Tier 2 skills. Spending time on foot skills outside of that would be much better spent on one of the topics in the different books of this series, in Tier 1, or in Tier 2 of this book.

This book and the other books in the series are meant to be read and understood, but also act as a guide to which you can refer back. Therefore, do not be afraid after you are done with this book to open it from time to time to have a refresher on the tips, tricks, tweaks, and techniques on improving your abilities. Now, keep in mind that a soccer player that wants to take their game to the next level will do whatever it takes to find the information that will help push him or her there. Then, he or she will implement the information in their practices to ensure it can be used in a game effectively.

The process of reading about how to become better, focusing on improving in practice, and then playing better in a game provides for continued growth and progress in any soccer player's career. However, be skeptical about some of the people creating YouTube videos. Many of the "soccer experts" that I have recently found on YouTube are showing poor form. This poor form results from people with little experience actually using the skills themselves in a game. This book provides a great opportunity to read the words to gain the knowledge needed to grow. Keep working to be the best player that you can be and I look forward to talking with you in the next book in the series.

Soccer Passing & Receiving:

A Step-by-Step Guide on How to Work with Your Teammates

Chapter 1

Speed of Play

In soccer, how fast your team can move the ball impacts your team's effectiveness. Although you do not always need to play at a high speed, letting the ball do most of the work will help save your team's legs so that you will have the stamina needed during the last minutes of a close game. **Using the speed of the ball will surely provide openings that would otherwise be absent.**

Take for example the Spanish national team from 2008 to 2012 and the Barcelona club team during a similar period. Both teams used the passing technique of Tiki-Taka (one or two touch passing) to wear down opponents, so that the other side would go for stretches of up to 10 minutes without even touching the ball. Forcing the other team to constantly play defense and chase the ball allowed the Spanish national team to win the Euro 2008, the 2010 World Cup and Euro 2012. Barcelona triumphed to the tune of six trophies in 2009 (Copa del Rey, League, Champions League, Spanish Super Cup, European Super Cup, Clubs World Cup). **The style of play involving considerable passing is excellent for reducing the hope of the other team when they barely have any time with the ball.** In fact, in a study published by *The Telegraph* on the English Premier League from the 2009/2010 season through the 2013/2014 season, the team with more possession won roughly 50% more often than the team with less possession.

To be a capable passer contributing to an increased speed of play, consider passing the ball into space. **Playing the ball into space helps teammates continue to run when they take their first touch on the ball**, which keeps your team's progress towards the other teams net. Additionally, move the ball out of high-pressure areas in your third and the middle third of the field to decrease the number of unnecessary turnovers by your team.

Think faster, act faster. In order to think more quickly, look around before you receive the ball so that you can plan your options. Also, practice the skills you will use in a game, so they become second nature and only need minimal thought. What separates good soccer players from the great soccer players is wisdom. Wisdom comes from experience. Therefore, one of the best ways to become better at soccer is to play it. However, keep in mind that it does not need to be your experience that provides you with the wisdom. **A wise person is one who can learn from others' mistakes and experiences.** Therefore, this book will help tremendously together with the constant desire to continue learning, which will help you grow into the soccer player you want to become. Learn from the soccer players you aspire to be like to reduce the time it takes to be the best.

In conclusion, to improve your speed of play, always look to pass the ball into space to continue a teammate's momentum. Passing into space helps you dictate the play even when you no longer have the ball. Have a plan to act faster when you receive the ball. Furthermore, keep developing your knowledge of the sport to refine your skills and abilities continually. Remember that the topics discussed in this book are situational and depend on the abilities of the opponent, the time remaining, the score, etc. Being able to make quality decisions is key and improving your knowledge of soccer is a quick way to decide on the best course of action during game situations.

Chapter 2

Passing with the Inside of Your Foot

As a soccer player, it is important to have the fundamentals down when it comes to passing. You can pass the ball with different parts of your foot, but the form that should be your most frequently used passing form is with the inside of your foot as follows:

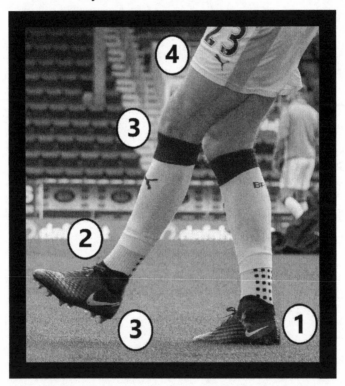

1. Plant next to the ball while pointing your foot and hips at your teammate
2. Toe up, heel down, and ankle locked
3. Knees slightly bent and foot slightly off the ground
4. Follow through after making contact with the ball

1. The form for a pass and shot are different. **With passing form, you can (and should) plant much closer to the ball because your body mechanics allow you to turn your leg and pass the ball with the inside of your foot.** Similarly to a shot, you want to have the leg that is planting on the ground pointed at the person or the open space to which you are passing the ball. You have your plant leg slightly bent, which is the same for your shooting form. You definitely do not want a straight leg when you will plant for a shot or a pass. Also, turn your hips towards the person or area on the field that you are passing the ball.

2. **Point your toe all the way up, which makes your heel go down.** Having your toe up and heel down naturally locks your ankle. Having a locked ankle will make it so that you have a powerful and more accurate pass. Also, locking your ankle allows the surface of the foot that you are passing the ball with (the side of your foot) to be wider. A more narrow foot creates more room for error so that if you miscalculate a little bit where the ball will be, you have a broader surface to make contact with the ball. Conversely, if your toe is pointed down and your heel is up, your ankle will be loose, resulting in a lack of power on your pass. Also, this makes your foot smaller and narrower, which means that your pass will be inaccurate if misjudged even slightly.

3. **Have the knee of your passing leg slightly bent.** You do not want a straight leg when you are passing. In fact, you do not want straight legs in most instances at all. When you straighten your leg and stand completely upright, you are not engaging the strongest muscle group of your legs, which is the quadriceps. This reduces your ability to be explosive with your shooting, passing, dribbling, running, jumping, etc. Having a bent leg naturally makes it so that your foot will be slightly off the ground. If you pass the ball with your foot touching the ground or close to the ground, the pass will result in the ball popping up in the air. Part of passing is to make sure that you are making it as easy as possible for your teammate. If you are consistently passing the ball in the air, you are making it more difficult for your teammates. Your teammates will likely then have to focus their first touch on bringing the ball to the ground before their second touch of the ball allows them to attack into space. Ideally, your pass should be firm, accurate, and on the ground so that their first touch can attack into space on the field.

4. **Next, make sure you follow through on your pass.** What you do with your leg after you completely follow through depends on the situation that you are in during the game, scrimmage, or practice. Most times, after you

make a pass, you will be running to another spot on the field to keep developing the play. Therefore, as you pass the ball (similar to a shot), you follow through and land on your passing foot. Then, you bring your back leg forward to take the next step. As you pass, you are already starting to continue to run and maintain your forward motion to the next spot on the field that you want to go. However, at times you will be passing the ball, while not being a part of the attacking portion of that play. For example, players that may do this are a goalie or in some instances, a defender. Therefore, you follow through after you pass the ball, but then you bring your leg back to where it began the passing motion. As a result, you end up in the same spot you started when you are making this pass.

Keeping your head down while you pass the ball keeps your chest over the ball and holds your form together for a more accurate pass. Having your head over the ball reduces the chance that the ball will pop up into the air when you pass the ball. As you may have noticed, this is an excerpt from the first book in the series, *Soccer Training*. This chapter is entirely related to passing and receiving, so it is included to make sure that you are able to read this important information in both books.

Chapter 3

The Weight of Your Passes

To ensure the ball gets to your teammates and that they can have a reasonable first touch, a soccer player must consider the weight of their passes. The weight of a pass is how hard or soft the passer plays the ball. How hard you pass the ball has a significant impact on whether your pass is intercepted, is received, or wasted because your teammate does not have enough time to react. Some of the considerations when passing are:

1. How far away is your teammate?
2. How much pressure is your teammate under?
3. How good at receiving passes is your teammate?

1. **The distance between you and your partner is key in the pace you have on your pass.** If your partner is only 5-7 yards from you, then you do not need to be concerned with having a powerful pass. In these instances, it is more important that you pass it to the correct foot or slightly in front of the correct foot, depending on the game situation. However, if your teammate is 20+ yards from you, softer passes will often be intercepted by a defender, so the pace of your pass is

critical. It needs to be powerful enough to ensure your team keeps possession.

2. **If your teammate has one or two defenders around them, then your pass needs to be harder because of an increased chance of the opposition interrupting the pass.** Though harder passes are more difficult to handle at short range, it is the responsibility of the teammate to control it or on you to find a better option. Attempt to lead your teammate out of pressure with your passes. If they have a person on their backside and one to their right, play the ball to their left to make it easier for them to find space.

3. **Consider the receiving abilities of the person you are passing the ball.** The better they are, the harder you can pass the ball, as they will be more likely to receive the ball skillfully. If the teammate that you are passing the ball to is not as coordinated, then pass it slower. If they are under pressure, then consider passing the ball to a different teammate altogether. Similarly, if you have better familiarity with your teammates so that they can anticipate what you will do and therefore react quicker, let this impact the weight of your pass too. Additionally, consider if you are passing to their dominant or opposite foot. Initially, assume a teammate or opponent is right-footed until you know otherwise.

Follow through on your passes to create greater accuracy and oftentimes, more power. Pass with the hardest part of the inside of your foot, near the heel, to increase the weight of the pass. Furthermore, swinging your leg faster will generate more power on your passes too. Increase the pace of the pass when a teammate is farther away, under pressure, and has good receiving skills. Pass it more softly when your teammate is closer, has little pressure, and is not good with his or her first touch.

Chapter 4

Masking Your Passes with the Outside of your Foot and Toes

In the second book of the Understand Soccer Series, *Soccer Shooting & Finishing: A Step-by-Step Guide on How to Score*, there is an entire chapter on shooting the ball with the outside of your foot and another chapter on shooting the ball with your toes. For this book, the form for passing with the outside of your foot or toes is very similar to using these forms to shoot, but the application of when to pass with the outside or toes of your foot are slightly different. Passing with the outside of your foot or your toes helps to mask your intentions, so the defense will not anticipate that you are making a pass when you do. To elaborate, an outside of the foot pass is extremely effective for the following reasons:

1. It is deceptive to the other team's defenders, midfielders, and forwards as to when you will pass the ball.

2. It creates a significant amount of curve, allowing you to pass around players on the other team.

From this image, use the bone of your foot, which is point "A". Additionally, **point the toe of your passing foot down and in, so that you may you use this portion of the foot to pass.** An outside of the foot pass is one of the most deceptive passes in the game. You pass the ball with the same portion of your foot that you would use if you were to dribble the ball. Therefore, it does not look like you will pass the ball most times when you go to actually pass it. Having a pass that does not look like a pass is terrific because most soccer players that pass the ball with an inside of the foot pass will find that defenders are often able to jump in front of the pass to intercept the ball. Since players on the other team often slide or lunge to be in front of the ball when you are passing, pass fakes are often very useful. If you pass and do not do a pass fake, it may result in the defender deflecting or stealing the ball when you attempt to pass it to a teammate. Often, this leads to a fast break for the other team.

Next, an outside of the foot pass is handy because it allows you to have a curve in the path that the ball takes. The curve is similar to that of a bent pass but often with more power similar to a driven pass. A bending pass is tremendous because the defender assumes you are still dribbling instead of passing, which increases the chances the pass is a success.

The outside of the foot pass allows you to diversify the way you can pass the ball to a teammate and continually keep the other team's players guessing. **When a defender knows you can use any part of your foot or can use either one of your feet, they tend to give you more space.** When they give you more space, it makes it even easier for you to have time to shoot, pass, dribble, or do whatever you need to do on the field. The defender will give you a certain amount of space and respect making your passing and receiving a little bit easier as the game goes on. Also, because your outside of the foot pass is going to be a bit curved, this enables you to find a passing lane that may not have been there otherwise.

Outside of the foot passes are very threatening when you are attacking down the sideline and cross the ball into the box before the defender even realizes what you are doing. Keep in mind that you should only develop the outside of the foot pass once you have become very comfortable with an inside of the foot pass and a driven pass. Please note that passing with the outside of your foot involves you turning your toes down and in to hit the ball with the laces of your cleats, which is directly on top of the bone of your foot. Performed this way, it allows you to place the hardest part of your foot on the ball to increase the power on your pass. Consider looking at Ricardo Quaresma for a great example of a player who effectively uses the outside of his foot.

When you first start playing soccer, you instinctively start off kicking the ball with your toe. You are quickly told that using a toe poke/toe blow is incorrect and that you should be using the inside of your foot to pass. In fact, many of my trainees have made fun of other trainees when they kick the ball with their toe. The trainees have been so conditioned that using their toe is incorrect, that they are confident enough to tease others who use it. However, after playing soccer with that limiting belief for the last 15 years, I have come across three instances that have entirely shifted my mindset over the last few years on why **a toe poke shot or pass can be great**.

First, when in a scrimmage against another team, the other team's coach had stopped his player after an attempt to score. The coach pulled the player and told him "when you are that close to the net, do not be afraid to toe poke/toe blow the ball if that is the only way you can take a shot. A shot with your toe is going to be a lot better than no shot at all." For me, the other team's coach drove home the message that taking more shots is going to result in more goals, even if they are not perfect shots. The chance may end up being a lucky and accurate shot, the goalie may mishandle the ball resulting in a goal, or the goalie may give up an easy rebound for you or a teammate to shoot the ball into the back of the net.

Second, it was a handful of years ago during "El Clásico" between the world's two largest soccer clubs: Barcelona and Real Madrid. The game ended in a draw because of Cristiano Ronaldo's goal. The average soccer fan watching simply saw that the ball went in the net. However, on closer inspection, a viewer could notice that the ball was played a little too far in front of Cristiano Ronaldo for him to shoot any other way than to use a toe poke/toe blow. This example points out that you can extend your leg further in front of you to reach the ball by using your toes to kick the ball, which means that you can reach further out and allow yourself to pass more often over your career when you understand that using your toe to pass is acceptable.

Third, a light bulb turned on while watching a highlight reel of outstanding goals. The only goal that stood out was Ronaldinho's goal, which says a lot since the video was several minutes long. Ronaldinho's goal was when he was still playing for Barcelona. On the YouTube video highlight reel, he scored from just outside the 18-yard box. He was standing still for a few seconds looking for a pass. The defender gave him as much time as he wanted as the defender felt he had stopped Ronaldinho from advancing with the ball or being able to shoot. The defender was standing in front of Ronaldinho and was waiting for him to make a move when suddenly, Ronaldinho decided to toe blow the ball, resulting in him scoring a goal.

If you have watched any of Ronaldinho's highlight videos before, then you have likely seen this goal and can imagine it right now. A key takeaway from this is that using a toe poke/toe blow creates deception that allows you to make a pass more efficiently. The defender was not expecting Ronaldinho's strike with his toes. The defender figured that it would be unrealistic for Ronaldinho to have any power on a shot given that he was standing still. The defender had it in his mind that he would either pass the ball or shoot a weak shot that the goalie could easily stop. However, Ronaldinho being the cheeky player that he is, thought of a simple and effective way to make the best out of the possible options he had available. He sought an opportunity to improve his team's chances of winning by toe poking/toe blowing the ball and took complete advantage of it. He was close enough to the net (on the 18-yard box) to have a toe blow as a viable option. If he were any further from the net, it would not have been reasonable to use his toe to strike the ball.

Therefore, by using the toe of your foot during appropriate game situations, it allows for three things that using the inside of your foot often does not:

1. It provides an additional way for you to make a pass. Make sure to strike the ball just below the center of the middle of the ball when doing a toe poke/toe blow.

2. It allows you to extend your leg so that you can make more passes by being able to reach further.

3. It is very deceptive to use a toe blow because most soccer players do not think that people will use their toe to kick a soccer ball, so it is misleading. You do not have to extend at the hip (only at the knee) as you would with the form for an inside of the foot pass, so it takes less time to

make a pass, which makes it very easy to disguise the pass.

One common trap that players fall into when it comes to passing with the outside of their foot is that they master passing with only their dominant foot and do not develop their opposite foot. The soccer player can compensate by just passing with the outside of their dominant foot instead of developing their opposite foot. An example of a player that relies exclusively on his dominant foot is Mesut Ozil. He spends energy and time avoiding his opposite foot that could be used to help his team score. Sadly, he is likely afraid to work on it for fear of failing, which is all too common with many soccer players. You probably will not make it as far as you want in your soccer career if you cannot use both of your feet. The number of opportunities in a game that exists for you to use your opposite foot is tremendous. Missing those opportunities during your entire career is detrimental for your confidence too.

Next, another outstanding way to mask your pass is to point towards an area of the field that you do not intend on passing towards. 9 times out of 10, the defender will take one or two steps towards that direction (the wrong direction) which gives you space in the direction that you either want to attack towards or make a pass.

Pointing is an advanced technique that takes no soccer skill on the ball, just a good sense of when to use it.

In conclusion, passing with the outside of your foot and your toes allows you to be deceptive to defenders and the goalkeeper. The outside of your foot allows you to bend the ball when you pass. Additionally, a toe blow pass is quicker than an inside of the foot pass, making a pass with your toe great to use after a shot fake or pass fake to ensure you can pass the ball past the defender. Master the inside of the foot pass before you spend a considerable amount of time on the outside of the foot pass or toe poke pass. It is an intermediate to an advanced level style of passing that can be made even better when you point, with your hand, in a different direction than you intend to pass.

Chapter 5
Effective Crossing

Effectively being able to cross the ball means that you can place in it in the area where a teammate can easily and efficiently take a shot or have a header on net. Not only do you have to worry about making it easy for a teammate but you also have to make it as difficult as possible for the other team's defenders and goalie to intercept, deflect, or clear your cross.

To start, when making a cross from the wing, **often the best area to cross the ball into is the "danger" area**. The danger area is between the 6-yard box and the penalty spot. A cross into the danger area is often too far in front of the goalie for him or her to react quick enough to grab the ball. This area is often behind the "backline" (the line across the field the defenders make), which places defenders in the compromised and risky position of having their bodies facing the net when attempting to clear a cross. The 2018 World Cup saw the most own goals ever scored in a World Cup because the players crossing the ball were so precise at delivering the ball into the danger zone. Keep in mind that the positioning of players is always changing.

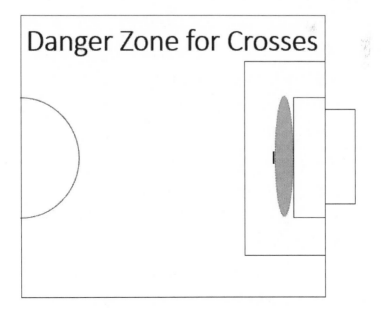

Danger Zone for Crosses

Therefore, the situation changes resulting in a need to revise your plan to score. However, a cross into the danger zone is often a much higher probability cross than other crosses. Make sure your teammates know this is where most your crosses will be, so they will give the effort to ensure they are in front of the net to score. One player that does a fantastic job of crossing the ball consistently into the danger zone is Kevin De Bruyne who plays for Manchester City and the Belgium National Team. Time after time he is making crosses into this area on the field, which explains why he is one of the top assisters if not the top assister each season in the league.

Next, driven crosses (fast crosses) leave the goalie less time to react but leave less time for a teammate to respond too. Generally, when you play a driven ball into the box, you want to play it no higher than waist level because it will be going too fast for a teammate to head the ball consistently. Additionally, driving it closer to the ground increases the chances that even if it is not an accurate pass, it may take a deflection and settle perfectly for a teammate to score.

Another cross to consider is the bent/curved cross. **Bent/curved crosses make it harder for the goalie to judge where the ball will be**, but it also makes it harder for a teammate to decide where the ball will be as well. A bent/curved cross will likely need to be lofted and is a great cross for teammates to score off of a header.

Keep the ball on the ground if your teammate has no defenders in front of him or her. Otherwise, loft the ball so they can shoot it or head it in. Why cross the ball, which forces your teammate to consider trapping the ball, before being able to shoot or pass? You can just as easily play them a pass that allows them to strike a one-time shot or take a useful attacking touch to help your team score.

Avoid switching the field in the air if your teammate has a defender on them. Unless you are under intense pressure, crossing the ball to a teammate with a defender on them will decrease the odds that your team maintains possession of the ball. Your team goes from you having 100% possession of the ball to you giving your teammate a 50-50 chance at winning the ball. Instead, consider looking for a closer teammate, so that you can make an accurate pass on the ground.

Try to avoid doing cross fakes when driving down one of the wings. Though it may work to fake out your defender, it will also fake out your teammates and result in them having poorly timed runs that can be easily countered by the other team. For example, you are dribbling with quick speed down the sideline and you have a defender in a foot race with you. You have teammates crashing the net expecting you to cross the ball when you pull your leg back, so they ensure that they are in what they believe are high probability spots for you to cross the ball. Just then, you decide to do a cross fake and all of your teammates are now correctly positioned if there were an actual cross, but too early given that you have not crossed the ball yet. After your cross fake, you immediately cross the ball, but your teammates have been standing in the correct position for a few seconds, which allows the defenders the time to properly cover your teammates. Now, your teammates have a much lower chance of being able to do anything with the ball and an increased chance of being offside.

Furthermore, it is often better to not even cross the ball if it is obvious that the other team's goalie will intercept the ball and if your entire team is on the opposition's half of the field. **Crossing the ball in this situation where the chances are great that the goalie will catch the ball, gives him or her a freebie to quickly start a counterattack against your team.**

In conclusion, be thoughtful when crossing. Understand that the danger zone is ideal for crosses, driven crosses need to be waist-level or lower, and bent crosses are ideal for a teammate to head the ball. When you want to cross the ball ultimately, avoid cross fakes, but know they are beneficial if your desire is to continue to dribble with the ball and not actually cross it.

Chapter 6

Should You Heel Pass?

Given that this book is about passing and receiving, one of the more common passing forms players use is attempting to pass the ball with their heel. A heel pass, when completed, can look wonderful. It is similar to that of an upper 90 shot. They both are low probability, but when they work, they look spectacular. **With that being said, heel passes have a low rate of success given that you are striking it with your heel.**

Furthermore, you are passing in a direction that you are no longer looking towards. There is an excellent chance that the ball will not be lined up perfectly towards your teammate's direction, which could result in it being easily intercepted by the defender. Also, for you to make a heel pass, you need to go from dribbling the ball while being behind the ball, to swinging your foot all the way in the front of the ball. Then, pulling your leg back, you can finally strike the ball with your heel. Heel passes take a considerable amount of time and it is easy for the defender to notice what you are doing and to step in front of the pass to intercept it. An intercepted pass in this scenario where you are going one way and passing it in the complete opposite direction will often result in the other team having a quick counterattack.

One famous soccer player that has used the heel pass on several occasions and has made himself look quite ridiculous in the process is the forward Mario Balotelli. Given that he is quite the showman, he likes to perform the low probability of success skills that look cool when completed. The problem is that because he performs skills that are unlikely to work, when he does not complete one of them, he often looks foolish.

He played in a game at the Herbalife World Football Challenge. He was in front of the net playing with Manchester City against LA Galaxy. He decided against making an easy pass to a teammate or even shooting the ball himself only 15 or so yards from the net. In fact, there was not a single defender in front of him or his teammate. He decided to fully rotate his body so that his back was facing the ball in order to strike the ball with his heel. He missed the net quite significantly. The entire fan base was in disbelief as well as the coach, who immediately substituted him out. Similarly, his teammates questioned his ability to make decisions and this was one of the many scenarios that led to his ultimate downfall from the heights that he had achieved in soccer.

In conclusion, heel passes are not that effective because it takes too long to strike the ball with your heel. To successfully complete a heel pass, you have to bring your leg fully in front of the ball, which is very obvious to the defender and often makes it easy for them to cut off the pass. Please understand that this is not to say that a heel pass should never be used, because there are those rare occasions when the ball rolls behind you and there is a clear passing lane to a teammate, but it should be used infrequently. Hitting the ball with your heel results in passes that are not likely to be accurate. Passes with your heel generally either give possession of the ball to the other team or place your teammate receiving the pass in a 50-50 situation. Neither are good when you are aiming to be an effective passer.

Chapter 7

Receiving the Ball

You can receive the ball with different parts of your foot, but the five general rules to receive a pass, listed in chronological order to ensure ball control and an accurate first touch are:

1. Plant next to the ball while pointing your foot and hips at your teammate
2. Toe up, heel down, and ankle locked
3. Knees slightly bent
4. Foot slightly off the ground
5. Typically, use the inside of the foot towards the heel to take an attacking touch

The form to receive a pass is the same as the first four steps of the form to make a pass. However, to receive a pass, there are a few more things to consider to make sure that you are productive with the ball:

1. **Demand the ball; do not ask for the ball. Yell for the ball; do not call for the ball.** These shifts in wording (demand versus ask and yell versus call) do a few excellent things for you as the person that wants to

receive a pass or be played a through ball. A through ball is when someone plays the ball in front of you and into space allowing you to run to the ball and continue your forward momentum at full speed.

Demanding the ball lets the person who is passing the ball know that you are very confident. It tells him or her that you will do something with the ball that is beneficial for your team. Think about it, if you are playing a game and have two people that you can pass the ball. The first person is screaming their head off demanding the ball. The other person is maybe showing for a pass, using a hand motion indicating that they want the ball, or meekly asking for the ball. Even if the person that is yelling for the ball is not quite as open, the player with the ball will consider passing to them because they can hear in their voice that they plan to do something with the ball. Also, demanding/yelling for the ball even if the person with the ball is close to you, ensures that he or she hears you.

Often, the person dribbling the ball is far away from you or potentially has a defender or two covering them. Therefore, by demanding/yelling for the ball, you let them know that you are open to receive the ball. **Many available passes in soccer are not made because the player with the ball did not know you were open.** They have their head down and looking at the ball, to protect the ball from the defender. If they do not hear you with their ears, they are not likely going to see you with their eyes. Lastly, yelling for the ball builds confidence in yourself and increases your ability to help your team achieve its offensive objective of scoring!

2. **Depending on the situation in the game, you want to make sure that you check to the ball (go towards the ball) in most instances.** More often than not, when you are receiving a pass, you should be checking to the ball to make sure that you successfully receive the ball. Waiting for the ball to travel to you risks a defender intercepting the pass. You definitely do not want to do that when you are making a "through" run and you want the pass played in front of you. In those situations, you want to communicate (yell/hand motion/or start sprinting in a direction away from the play, but down the field) to them where you are going and let them pass the ball in front of you so that you can take your first touch in stride.

One of the more frustrating things for a coach and a teammate is when you are passed a good (not a great) pass and you are not able to receive the ball because you are playing lazily. You must be active, on your toes, and going to receive the pass. If you do not, it allows the defender to come between you and the ball. This laziness results in an intercepted pass, which makes it very easy for the other team to have a counterattack due to you losing possession during a simple pass.

3. **Before receiving a pass, make sure to scan the field and look behind you.** Having a good idea of what you plan to do before you actually do it will make you a much more effective soccer player and teammate. It does not have to be a 5 to 10-second scan. It is just a quick swivel of the head to see if there is pressure and where some open teammates are for you to make a sensible pass or dribble in space after you receive the ball. A quick look is something that sets college players apart from high school players and definitely professional players from college players.

These differences are things that coaches and scouts notice. An excellent defender, midfielder, or striker will know where teammates and opponents are on the field. Therefore, as they are receiving the pass, they are already thinking about what their next actions in the game will be. In soccer and life, if you fail to plan, you plan to fail. **By quickly scanning behind you, you are already starting to give yourself time to develop a plan of attack.** The fast scan will surely help you score more often or let you deliver the pass that will allow your team to score.

4. **Next, when you receive a pass in most game situations, you still want your hips to be square with your teammate.** Though when you are along a sideline this advice may change, being squared with your teammate means that you are pointing your hips at your teammate. When your hips are square with your teammate, you will be more accurate with your first touch than if your hips are not pointing at your teammate. In this instance, you are creating an L with your stance by pointing your plant foot at your teammate. The foot that you are receiving the pass with is turned, so you can use the inside of your foot to take your first touch. This form is basically the same as if you were making a pass.

5. **Roughly 95% of your first touches in a game should be attacking touches.** An attacking touch pushes the ball into space with your first touch. An attacking touch is the alternative to taking a touch where the ball stops at your feet. An attacking touch may go towards your opponents net, towards your own net, or in any direction away from where a defender can reach the ball. In a game, you should mostly be taking attacking touches because it allows you, with your first touch, to already have the ball going in the direction that you want to take it.

More often than not, the first attacking touch is into space on the field to give yourself more time to think, to pass, to dribble, to shoot, to do whatever you need to do with the ball. Next, by taking the first step with your attacking touch, you will have a more accurate first touch. Looking at the picture, use part "B" to take an attacking touch with the hardest part of your foot, which can be referred to as the "bat."

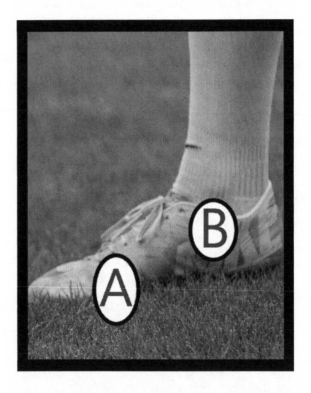

Your attacking touch is not meant to push the ball really far away from you; it is intended for you to take your first step in the direction that you want to go. **An attacking touch was something I did not realize for the longest**

time that is a key to being a fast soccer player. I thought that you had to be a quick runner to be a fast soccer player. In reality, you have to be great with your first attacking touch to be a fast soccer player. This one tip alone changed my game overnight. The attacking touch helps your acceleration tremendously because you are already starting to build momentum and speed in the direction that you want to go, which enables you to distance yourself from the defender who is marking you.

6. **Occasionally, it will be appropriate to take a touch underneath your body (a touch that stops at your feet).** This touch is necessary when you have too many people around you and someone could easily cut an attacking touch off and take possession of the ball from you. Only then is it okay to take your first touch under your body. Also, if you receive a difficult pass, ideally you still take an attacking first touch, but it is understandable if you take a first touch that stops underneath you and then start attacking with the ball. Bad passes are generally ones played to you in the air. Looking at the picture again, use part "A" to take a touch with the softest portion of your foot, which can be referred to as the "broom" to settle the ball at your feet.

7. When you move to receive the pass, what you plan to do next with the ball determines which portion of your foot

to use to take an attacking touch. **Ideally, the attacking touch will really be an attacking step.** You push the ball with the same portion of your foot (the inside of your ankle) that you pass a ball with because it will be locked to push the ball better. However, if you want the ball to stop underneath you, take your first touch with the inside of your foot up towards your toes.

There is space in your shoe between your toes, there is a lot more fabric, and a lot less bone towards your toes. This area of your foot is your "broom" and because your "broom" is not very hard, the ball will stop underneath you. Look at the portion of the foot labeled "A" in the previous image. Additionally, if you want your first touch to go completely behind you so that you can accelerate away from pressure and into space, then you can take the touch even more softly towards the inside of your foot using your toes (using the "broom"). Do this more softly than if you wanted to stop the ball underneath you. The softer touch ensures that the ball does not go racing by you. You slow it down a little bit, but do not stop it entirely because you want to be attacking in the space directly behind you.

Chapter 8

Receiving with the Correct Foot

To be a productive player on the field, you want to make soccer as easy as possible for you and as hard as possible for the opposing team. One way to increase the chances of your success is to receive the ball with the correct foot. Now, understand that this advice is not for 100% of circumstances, but can be used in many game situations, so that you can quickly fire a shot, play a pass, or dribble the defender.

To start, you generally want to receive with the foot that is in the direction that you want to go. Specifically, if you are looking to attack to the left, receive the ball with your left. If you are going to the right, then take your first touch of the ball with your right foot. Doing this allows your first touch to be a first step in the direction that you are looking to go, enabling you to already start generating some momentum. On the contrary, if you wanted to attack to your left, but took your first touch with your right foot, you would naturally have to cross your feet. Crossing your feet is generally regarded as unathletic. Furthermore, your touch will often be less accurate because you will often turn your hips too much when crossing your feet. So instead of a consistent touch in the direction that you want to go, you will have crossed feet and semi-accurate first touches.

Next, the general rule mentioned in the previous paragraph applies when you have your back facing the net you need to score in as well. **However, when attacking forward, you want to use the inside of your foot and when you want to attack behind you, use the outside of your foot to push the ball.** When taking that attacking first touch, make it the first step too. As mentioned previously, it generates momentum in the direction you plan to go. Your step also increases your accuracy naturally creating a follow through to ensure the ball goes in the direction you desire it to travel.

Remember, this is not advice for every situation, but is applicable for roughly 90% of the time. There may be situations when you are a forward with a defender on your backside who has been preventing you from turning the entire game or you are a midfielder in a crowded area of the field, when it may be more appropriate to receive the ball differently. However, crossed legs create less accurate touches and are not a risk worth taking often when playing.

When receiving the ball, using the correct foot will add speed to your game by creating time and space for you. When you need to place a touch several yards away, take the touch towards the heel on the inside of your foot, as this is a harder portion of your foot and will make the ball travel further. If you are in a high-pressure area with seemingly countless opponents surrounding you, then a touch with the inside of your foot towards the toes is ideal to settle the ball close to you, since the toes are the softer portion of your foot. Use the correct foot and the correct portion of your foot for the situation to become the great soccer player you want to be!

Chapter 9

Know Before You Receive the Pass

Soccer players generally reside in one of two groups. The first is that they react to what is happening to them on the field. The second group is made up of those who plan and act on that plan. The first type of player is often the one that only scores a couple of goals a season and is also the player that is often lacking confidence on the field. The second type of soccer player is the person that leads the team in goals or assists, is looked at by their teammates for direction, and often plays every single minute of the game. Let us dive into what it takes to be a proactive player instead of a reactive player:

1. Take a quick look
2. Make a plan
3. Revise the plan as needed

1. Take a quick look over your shoulder when you are receiving the ball with your back facing the net you need to score in. **Looking up quickly before you receive a pass makes it easy to form a picture in your mind of where nearly everyone is on the field.** This image of the placement of teammates and opposition allows you to decide on your plan of action, even while you are not

looking at where you plan to go. Notice when professionals play, they take a quarter of a second look to dramatically improve their performances. Additionally, looking at the field before you receive the ball provides confidence on the ball because you know how heavily the other team is currently pressuring you.

2. Make a plan of how to proceed once you receive the ball. More often than not, you will not be passed the ball, so you will have to be continually revising your plan as you await a pass. Your positioning, the defense's form, and the person attempting to pass the ball changes, so you need to adapt quickly. Now, you do not need a detailed plan for every dribble you take, but you do want a general idea of what you plan to do.

For example, you are standing in the middle of the field as a midfielder and you turn your head just before receiving the ball. You realize that there is pressure behind you to your right, but space to your left. Therefore, as the pass is played to you, you should take a step towards the ball so the defender does not intercept it. With your first touch, you guide the ball behind you to your left. It is as simple as that! Once you guide the ball there, then you take a quick look up and see if anyone is making a quality run, or if there is a forward checking to the ball that is open. Again, it is very simple. You made two plans in virtually no time. **Remember, these plans do not have to be rocket science, just you knowing what your next one or two moves are before you do them makes you much more effective.**

Another situation to mention is if you are a forward receiving a pass from a midfielder, you turn to look as you are checking to the midfielder, which allows you to realize that an outside midfielder is starting to make a run down the side of the field where there is a ton of space. Since you see they are creating a great opportunity, instead of trying to turn with the ball, you can play a one-touch pass. One more instance is if you are an outside defender receiving a pass from your goalkeeper. As he or she is passing you the ball and you are checking to it, you take a quick look up the field to see a forward from the other team sprinting towards you. Excitedly, you one-touch it back to the keeper so they can go either up the field or to the other outside back with a pass. Seriously, all it needs to be is a one or two-step plan when you receive the ball.

The reason why coming up with a plan is essential is because visualizing your passes, foot skills, shots, etc. is nearly as effective as having practiced them once before. Creating a quick plan is roughly 70% equivalent to already having once done what you are about to do. This visualization is key for acting upon others instead of reacting to others. Acting versus reacting is the difference between a team leader and a bench warmer.

3. Ideally, when you make a plan, everything will work exactly as you imagined it. However, this is rarely the case, which is why it is so **important that you revise your plans quickly as you see different situations develop on the field.** Generally, you know how other players on your team and the other team will react, but more often than we would like, they do not do as expected. If you read to learn more about what opposing players are supposed to be doing and they do something different, this allows you to take advantage of this situation.

In conclusion, take a look to see what options are available. Then, make a short plan for what your intentions are. Afterward, keep following the plan until your assumptions change and you need to create a new plan or you have passed the ball to a teammate. At this point, make another plan. Do not overthink the plans, just keep a few key points in mind such as attack into space when receiving a pass, yell for the ball when you are open, and look for high probability passes. This will ensure that you are a terrific passer on your team.

Chapter 10

Find a Passing Lane

Something that players and coaches cannot stand from a team member is someone who expects perfect passes over or under the opposition. It is your personal responsibility to get open for them to pass the ball directly to you with ease. Now this is not to say a difficult pass should never be made. However, roughly 90% of your passes should be ones that you are very confident will make it to a teammate. (Obviously, if time is running out towards the end of the game and your team is losing, then you should consider more difficult passes if your options are limited).

If you do not initially receive the pass from your teammate, then KEEP MOVING to move into a better position for them to pass you the ball. It is likely that from their point of view you are not in an excellent position to receive the pass or you have not opened your mouth to let your teammate know you are open. One incorrect belief that plagued me during my youth was that I would not call for the ball. I thought that my teammate should dribble with his head up so that he could see me if I was open because if I called for the ball, the other team would know I was open.

The problem with the mindset of not calling for the ball was that my teammates often dribbled with their head down, which meant the ball was rarely passed to me. My incorrect mindset meant very few goals and very few assists a season for me because this limiting belief reduced the number of times I touched the ball. Additionally, calling for the ball will often draw a defender towards you, which can reduce the amount of pressure your teammate has. Therefore, be both assertive and a great team player at the same time. "Assertive" in a sense that you want the ball, while drawing pressure to create space to help decrease the number of the other team's players closing in on your teammate.

One favorable way to ensure that you can find a quality passing lane is to be deceptive with your runs. **A deceptive run is one in which you take two or three steps in one direction and then explode in a different direction.** A deceptive run is extremely beneficial because it can help create space that would have otherwise not been there. Starting a deceptive run will often require the defender to follow you. The exciting thing is that you know your intentions of a sneaky run, but he or she does not. Therefore, with your first two or three steps, they will start covering you, requiring them to begin to run too. This means their momentum will be carrying them the wrong way when you decide to change your direction. In the first book in the Understand Soccer Series, *Soccer Training*, we discussed how hard and time consuming it is for a defender to go from running in one direction, stopping their bodies, and then going in another direction.

A standout player who comes to mind when talking about making quality runs is Cristiano Ronaldo. He can consistently score the tap in goals and headers that most other players cannot because he knows how to make a quality run. His height and pace surely help too but would be nothing if he did not know where to go to increase his chances of receiving the ball in front of the net.

In summary, be a player that does not expect perfect passes through the reaching legs of multiple defenders. Know that a spectacular ball in the air that is hard enough to prevent a player on the other team from intercepting the ball, soft enough for you to take a comfortable first touch, and in the perfect spot based on your run is more often than not an unreasonable request. Find passing lanes that are more reasonable to pass in and can ensure your team maintains possession to keep on the offensive. The bonus to remaining on the attack is that most players find they use more energy running after a ball the other team is passing than having possession themselves. Wear the other team out with runs into passing lanes that are made available by deceptive starts and demand the ball from your teammate to help relieve some of their pressure and increase your chances of receiving the ball.

Chapter 11

Tell Your Teammate Where You Want the Ball

Do not expect the pass that you want if you are unable to tell the person passing the ball exactly where you want it. **Point with your hands.** A suggestion is to open your hand in front of you if you want the ball at your feet, open your hand to the right if you want it slightly in front of you to your right, or open your hand to the left if you want it slightly in front of you to the left. Point to the spot on the field if you want the ball played well in front of you, so that you may sprint to the ball.

Make sure you communicate these hand signals to teammates to make this process easier and so they know what you want in a pass. Expressing where you want the ball is one of those skills that take no soccer abilities with the ball whatsoever. **Think about it, there are several things that you can do to increase your ability to receive a good pass, most of which are just as easy for you to do as they are for you not to do.**

Showing a teammate where you want the ball is most easily done during throw-ins, set pieces, and goal kicks. Point to where you want the ball, but point using your hand in a way that allows your teammate to see where you want the ball, but the person covering you cannot. For example, if you have a defender behind you, point using your thumb, but position your hand in front of you, so the defender cannot see where you want your teammate to pass the ball. Keep in mind that if you are doing this on the run, there likely is not enough time for a fellow midfielder or forward to fully look where you are pointing your thumb, so this is better reserved for when you are a forward or midfielder asking for the ball from a defender who has minimal pressure on him or her.

To summarize, let your teammate know you want the ball by demanding it (not asking for it) and yelling for it (not calling for it). Yell for the ball when you think you have a better chance of keeping possession or attacking. Use your hands to help you and your teammate be on the same page, which increases the chance that there is a successful pass. Keep in mind that the reverse works too. If you are the one with the ball, do not be afraid to point where you want your players to be, either to ensure you will pass it to them or to create space for someone else.

Chapter 12

Receiving the Ball Out of the Air

Ideally, when passes are played to you, they are on the ground. However, this will not happen all of the time. Occasionally, you are played a pass through the air. **Taking a great touch out of the air depends on the pressure of the defense and how high the ball is played to you.**

If the ball is played to you in the air while you are under high pressure, then use the front of your

shoulder or your forehead to take an attacking first touch in the direction you need to go. Obviously, this is easier said than done and takes practice to master. Using your forehead or shoulders is ideal to take the attacking touch of the ball out of the air.

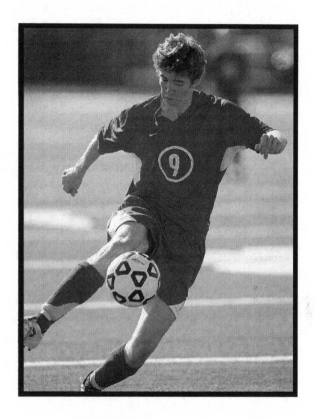

When the ball is played in the air and you have time to control it, allow it to hit the ground just slightly before pushing the ball in a direction you want to go. Using the inside of the foot as an example, when the ball is passed to you in the air, judge where the ball will land. Once you can see roughly where it will hit the ground, position yourself at that spot. **Then, as the ball hits the ground and starts to bounce up into the air, position the inside of your foot just over the ball so that it bounces into your foot.** The ball bouncing into your foot will push it back towards the ground. Trapping the ball this way allows you to successfully trap the ball out of the air in a way that takes as few touches as possible and lets you continue attacking with speed.

Keep in mind that using the inside of your foot towards your toes will create a small touch because your toes are the softest portion of the inside of your foot. **For a touch out of the air that allows you to take a large attacking touch in the direction you want to dribble, use the inside of your foot towards your heel.** This portion of your foot is harder and will make for a touch that travels significantly further.

Additionally, one mistake trainees often make is leaning back when taking a touch from a pass in the air after the ball just hit the ground. Tilting back changes the angle of your foot making it easy for the ball to go right, left, upwards, or forward. Obviously, you want more certainty in your touch and the direction the ball travels. Therefore, have your body, shoulders, and chest over the ball, so that even if your touch is not perfect, it will remain in front of you. As previously mentioned, if you mistakenly lean back, then it makes it likely for your first touch to be into the air and it could go left, right, in front of you, or even up and over you.

In conclusion, when under significant pressure, take your first touch of ball played in the air with either your forehead or shoulder. When you have a bit more space, let the ball hit the ground and just as it starts to bounce up, have the inside of your foot there to push it back towards the ground. Keep your shoulders over the ball while doing this to increase the accuracy of your first touch. Leaning back shows you are not confident to receive the ball and will create a first touch that could end up going in many directions. Also, do not forget that leaning backwards can leave you off balance when you are looking to take your next touch or step.

Chapter 13

Turning with a Defender on Your Back

As a soccer player who is looking to receive passes, you will often find yourself with your back turned towards the very thing you are aiming to score in, the other team's net. **It is incredibly important that you are able to effectively receive a pass, turn your body with the ball, and explode up the field.** Ideally, you should be able to do this all in one motion. Recently, this topic was the main focus of a training session for one of my trainees, Kylie Kade, who has aspirations of playing for the United States Women's National Team. Steps to consider when turning with a defender on your backside are:

1. Look over your shoulder before you receive the pass to determine if you have space and believe you can do something productive for your team. (Have your head on a swivel.)

2. Keep your arm out to help you balance and prevent the opposing team's defender from going around you to cut off the pass.

3. Either have your shoulders pointed directly at the ball when it is coming towards you (so that you are not showing which way you are going) or be tricky by using your body to fake like you are going one way when you are planning to push the ball in the other direction.

4. Use the outside of your foot to push the ball. It is not just a first touch you are looking to take but a first step that includes the first touch, so that you can accelerate away more quickly from the defender.

First, it cannot be stressed enough that you should look behind your shoulder when you are preparing to receive a pass. Depending on the situation, it may be best to just hold the ball and wait for support. A quick look will allow you to know where you should push the ball or even if you should request a pass at all from a teammate. **Do not twist at the hips to look behind you because this takes too much time.** Only turn your head by using your neck to make sure that you can take a swift look at the field and the players behind you. If you do this and determine that you have space to attack then yell for the ball and demand that it be passed to you.

Second, as a soccer player, you will very rarely be called for having your arm touching an opponent. As such, when you are ready to receive the pass with your back facing the net you are looking to score in, **keep your arm up for balance, but especially to hold back the defender to ensure you are the one to receive the pass and not the other team.** Having your arm up does not mean that you should hold onto them, but you should place your forearm against them to slow their attempt to travel around you to intercept the ball. Also, having your arm up allows you to feel where the defender is, which factors into your decision on how to turn.

Third, never show the defender where you are going by revealing it to him or her with your body. When turning with your back to the goal and a defender is behind you, either have your shoulders pointed directly at the ball when it is coming towards you or be deceptive and use your body to fake like you are going one way when you are planning to push the ball in the other direction. **Having your body pointed directly at the ball does not reveal to the defender which way you are going**, which is good, but the defender will only commit to going in a direction that they believe you will be pushing the ball. This is why it is so effective to use your body to pretend like you are going one way, while your real intentions are to go the other way.

Therefore, have your shoulders turned slightly in the direction that you want your defender to think

you are going. Many defenders read the opposing player's body language as much as they read where the ball is currently located when judging how to stop an attacking player with the ball. Therefore, if you show the defender the direction that you are not going, they will often overcommit to the wrong side. If the defender commits to the wrong side, it will make it very easy for you to dribble past the defender without worrying about slowing down the speed of play or having the defender steal the ball.

When taking a deceptive first touch, there are two options. First, if you are looking to take your first touch in the space to the area behind you to the right, then turn your body/shoulders slightly to the left (so the defender will assume you are going to the left) and raise your right leg so it looks like you will be pushing to the left. However, at the last second, before receiving the pass, move your right leg across your body so that you can push with the outside of your foot to go to the space behind you to the right. Do the opposite of this if you looking to go to the space behind you on the field, to the left. The second option for when you want to deceive a defender into thinking you are going to the area to the left behind you when you are really looking to go to the right is to start by pointing your body/shoulders slightly to the left, then look as if you will push the ball with your left foot.

However, pretend to push the ball with your left foot a bit too early, so that you can plant that left leg on the ground, and raise your right leg across your body to push the ball with the outside of your right foot. Think of this as a jab/feint where you miss receiving the ball with your left foot and take it with your right. You can choose which move suits you better. The first option takes some flexible ankles and the ability to pivot with the plant foot that is already on the ground. The second option provides a very stable plant of the left foot just after you have purposely missed the ball to allow for quick acceleration out with your right foot. Therefore, the second option is my preferred option, but please try both and see which one feels better and is quicker for you.

Fourth, it is ideal to use the outside of your foot to push the ball when turning into the space diagonally behind you because it allows you to take your first touch/step without having your legs crossed when you plant to explode away. Crossing your legs is very unathletic and should be avoided when possible as it is hard to explode with speed and it is easier to become unbalanced. It is especially important to be active and on the toes/balls of your feet to be ready for any pass.

To take a smaller touch when turning with a defender on your backside, take your first touch/step with the outside of your foot toward your toes because this is a softer area on your foot and the ball will not bounce off as powerfully. For a bigger touch, use the portion of your outside foot towards your heels to push the ball since this is hardest area of the outside of your foot. Push the ball far enough to create space between you and the defender.

Combine the four steps of check over your shoulder, lift your arm for balance and to prevent the defender from intercepting your pass, point your shoulders towards the person passing, and push the ball with the outside of your foot where the leather meets the laces. These steps will help you become a deceptive forward that is quickly able to make progress up the field, even if your back is turned to it. Turning with your back towards the net is a skill that many soccer players never learn. However, if this skill is mastered, it will place you in an elite class of forwards that are confident and able to control the ball. Several players that are known for their ability to be a point man (a big presence capable of winning balls out of the air and connecting passes for smaller/quicker players) are Karim Benzema, Edinson Cavani, Gonzalo Higuaín, Olivier Giroud, and Zlatan Ibrahimović.

Chapter 14

How to Shield the Ball

It is crucial that you can protect the ball to ensure that you can distribute the ball to your teammates as necessary. To shield the ball appropriately, consider the following three things:

1. Have a low center of gravity
2. Spread your arms
3. Push the ball away from pressure

1. When shielding the ball while there is a player from the opposite team behind you, **it is vital that you have a lower center of gravity than the opponent that is reaching in for the ball.** A lower center of gravity will give you a solid foundation and make it nearly impossible for the other player to move you and take possession of the ball. Your center of gravity is how high your hips are from the ground, so within reason, bringing your hips down several inches will make it so that you are more stable and more difficult to push off the ball. This positioning is similar to that of a quarter squat where you squat 1/4th of the way down. This position is optimal to shield the ball from the other team.

2. **Have your arms out.** Having your arms out means both extending at the shoulder and at the elbow to make your body and your arms as wide as possible. Though you may have been taught from a young age that you are not supposed to have your elbows or even your arms up, the referees will hardly ever call you for having your arms raised, especially when you are shielding the ball from a player on the other team. Using your arms as leverage to make it more difficult for the opposition to steal the ball increases the chance that you will effectively shield the ball and be able to pass it to a teammate. Having your arms out naturally makes you wider and therefore it will take longer for the defender to travel around you and your

arms to steal the ball. Even if the defender does, you would likely take a touch away from them to buy you more time. Use the area on your arm between your wrist and elbow to make contact and provide the best mechanical advantage while giving enough space between the ball and the defender.

3. When shielding a ball, it is crucial that you are not afraid to take a touch away from pressure. **A touch away from pressure will help generate some momentum, as well as buy more time to decide on how or if you will pass the ball to a teammate.** If a player on the other team is coming to your right side behind you, then push the ball more towards the left. Having the ball on the opposite side from the opposition allows you to keep your body entirely between the ball and the other team's player.

Obviously, your size and the size of your opponent makes a difference. If you are 5'5" and you are going up against someone that is 6'5," you will find that their leg length and natural strength will make it very difficult for you to shield the ball. **If you are at a significant size disadvantage, avoid situations where you may be required to shield the ball.**

In conclusion, keep your center of gravity low by going a quarter of the way down into a squat. Spread your arms out at the shoulder and the elbow, so they are wide and away from you. Move the ball away from pressure to prolong the time that you are able to shield the ball correctly. Watch Philipp Lahm, the German National Team star and Bayern Munich player, for a great example of a small player that follows the advice in this chapter to effectively shield the ball from his opponents.

Chapter 15

Examples of Corner Kick Set Plays

A corner kick is where someone on your team will need to pass the ball and hopefully someone from your side will receive the ball. As a result, let us discuss helpful positioning and a few set plays for corners to ensure your passing and receiving skills are on point.

In general, if you are a defender looking to score or produce an assist, position yourself towards the corner of the 18-yard box nearest the corner where the kick is being taken from. **Consider positioning yourself just outside the 18-yard box to intercept and shoot any clearance attempts by the other team.** This positioning helps for various reasons. First, it gives the person taking a corner kick a potential person to pass the ball. However, it is often recommended that the person taking the corner kick crosses the ball into the box because a mistake by the defense or a deflection will allow your team to have a close-range shot. However, if your team is severely disadvantaged when it comes to height, then consider passing it to the person at the corner of the 18-yard box and avoid making what would likely be a wasted cross.

Next, being the defender towards the corner of the 18-yard box nearest the corner kick is beneficial because more often than not, when a defender is clearing the ball, it will end up being cleared to this spot. Defenders do not often look behind themselves during a corner kick to be comfortable with heading the ball to the other side of the field from which the corner kick came. Also, the other team's defenders do not want to head the ball to the top of the 18-yard box, because they know a member of the other team will be standing there, waiting for a cleared ball to fire a shot at the net. Therefore, they can either clear it out on the goal-line, which gives your team another corner kick or towards the top corner of the 18-yard box, which is ideally where a defender on your team is placed.

When it comes to midfielders, if you are taller or have a good vertical leap, then definitely position yourself in the box to attempt a header. However, keep in mind that you must row your arms back and extend your neck and head forward to hit the ball with your forehead to have the most powerful header possible. **Power is emphasized since headers are not scored often when they lack enough speed to travel past the goalkeeper.** If you are shorter, then consider going toward the top of the 18-yard box in case the ball comes out to you, so that you may strike it. Alternatively, be towards the wing opposite of where the corner kick is being taken in case the ball sails over nearly everyone's head. Keep in mind that as a midfielder, you have defensive responsibilities too, so unless you are really good at using headers, being in the 6-yard box will not be too advantageous.

Lastly, as a forward, your primary job is to score! Therefore, you better be in the box looking to get a head, knee, or foot on the ball. You have minimal defensive responsibilities, so feel free to screen the goalie to make it easier for your teammates to score and look for deflections and rebounds in front of the net.

A terrific corner kick play is one that is mentioned in the second book of the Understand Soccer Series: Soccer Shooting & Finishing. **This corner involves a quick restart where you grab the ball as quickly as it goes out, place it on the corner spot and have previously communicated to a teammate, so they make a run from the top of the 18-yard box to the near post to take a quick shot.** Even if they do not score from this angle, which they often will, there is often a rebound that another player on your team can shoot the ball into the back of the net. In fact, in a recent game, I was taking the corner kick. I sprinted to grab the ball, placed it on the corner spot and without even taking a step back, I played a pass on the ground towards the penalty spot. This is a pre-planned corner for one of my teammates and me. He fired a successful shot towards the far post for a spectacular and much-needed goal to tie a team we were initially losing 3 to 0 against. Quick corner kicks often catch the other team off guard.

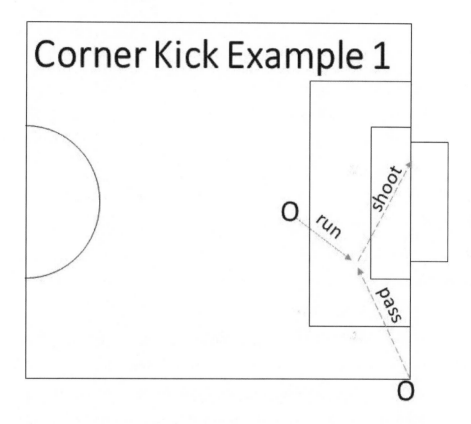

Corner Kick Example 1

When you do not have any set plays established on your team, the ideal spot to place the ball is the penalty spot. The penalty spot is often further than the goalie is willing to travel, but still close enough to the net that there is a chance that you can score from a header. If the ball drops in that area, even better as it gives you a straight on shot to score.

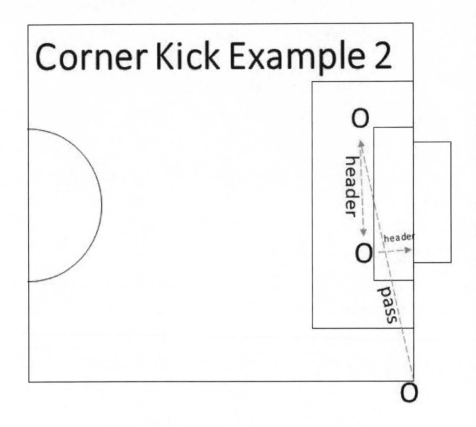

Corner Kick Example 2

Finally, here are the details for a corner kick that takes a bit more coordination and is definitely an advanced level corner kick, as shown in the image. **Play a ball to a person on your team that is past the far side of the net.** That person then heads it to the post nearest where the corner kick was taken. Make sure this has been previously communicated so a teammate will be there. Enjoy the outcome of this play, which is often a goal without a goalie directly in front of you. The initial cross draws the goalkeeper to the post farthest from where the corner was taken. Therefore, when the ball is headed to the near post, the goalie may be stuck at the far post. The person at the near post will have an easier time scoring.

Even if the first header is not as accurate as the teammate receiving the pass needs, **the ball will still be in a dangerous spot in front of the net where the goalie is several steps away from.** When playing a corner into the 18-yard box, it is best to have a bent cross. Similarly to the fast restart, the bent shot/cross is discussed in the second book in the series, so check it out for detailed steps on performing it. Bent crosses are useful for corner kicks because they are difficult for the goalie to judge. Furthermore, they are lofted enough to travel over the other team's player that will likely be positioned as the first line of defense at the corner of the 6-yard box closest to where the corner is being taken. Conversely, you can take the corner kick short and have a person at the near post flick the ball to the far post.

In conclusion, the corner kick is a terrific chance for you to showcase either your passing or receiving skills. Adjust where you are for the corner kick based on your size, abilities, and what position you are playing on the field when you are not taking a corner kick. When you are the person taking a corner kick, either rely on a pre-planned set-piece or kick the ball towards the high probability area of the penalty spot.

Chapter 16

Examples of Throw-In Set Plays

Similarly to corner kicks, throw-ins offer a fantastic opportunity for you and a teammate to work on your passing and receiving skills. **To start, you likely know that you have to have both feet on the ground. You need to bring the ball back behind your head.** As you bring the ball forward, release it to pass the ball to a teammate. Therefore, let us dive into some of the unique things to consider when either taking a throw-in or being the person looking to receive a throw-in.

When you are the person taking a throw-in, you ideally want your throw-in to go towards a teammate's foot. This will allow them to take an attacking first touch immediately instead of having to settle a ball that has been thrown to their chest or head. For example, when I was in high school, I considered a successful pass as one that traveled to my teammate. Not until late into my senior year of playing varsity soccer for one of the largest Division 1 schools in the state did a teammate tell me that I needed to keep my passes down.

He explained that they were difficult to control and that a pass in the air that could have just as easily been played on the ground should not be considered a successful pass. At first, due to a fixed mindset, I was a bit offended that he was trying to correct the way I played. Then, after a considerable amount of time thinking about his comments, I realized that he was absolutely right and that a pass to a person's chest or head just was not good enough. As a result, I was able to better see when other teammates would make passes that looked similar to that and I now knew to avoid being a soccer player who set my teammates up for a greater chance of failure.

Too many of my teammates over the years had thrown the ball to my chest or head when there were only a few yards between us. Make it easy on your teammate if there is no defender between you and them. Have your throw-in travel towards their feet instead. This allows them to control the ball on the ground quickly by taking an attacking touch with their first touch instead of worrying about settling the ball. **If it takes two touches to go from where you initially stand during a throw-in, to where you want to go, you likely will not get the luxury of a second touch without it being met by a defender's foot attempting to poke the ball away.**

Next, as the person taking the throw-in, avoid playing to someone with multiple players covering them. Remember, a throw-in down the field may result in a turnover, but it is much safer than playing the ball back to a defender on your team who has a forward covering them. **Find the open person, the person demanding**

the ball, or space on the field that a teammate starts to run towards.

Also, play the ball backward if your defender is open. Occasionally, you do not have time to go backward or you just do not trust your defender to do something productive with the ball. Avoid the defense in these situations, but **an open defender is often the easiest way to maintain possession on throw-ins.**

Additionally, an outstanding way for you, the person taking the throw-in, **to create space for your teammates is to fake one way, then throw the ball where you actually want it to go.** The other team will shift momentarily to cover where they initially believe you are throwing the ball, likely opening up space where you really plan to throw-in the ball. To do this effectively, do not scan the field by moving your head when you go to take a throw-in, but scan the field as you are going to collect the ball. When the ball is in your hands, point your hips in a direction you do not want the ball to go, then quickly adjust your foot stance to turn your hips to take a throw-in that catches the other team off guard.

More often than not, you will be the person looking to receive a throw-in than the person actually taking the throw-in. Something to consider when looking to increase the chance of a teammate throwing you the ball is to not immediately set up where you want the ball. **Make a 2-3**

step run in the wrong direction and then explode into open space that you just created to give your teammate an excellent option to throw you the ball. The person throwing in the ball will appreciate you making their job easier. Furthermore, your change of speed shows the person throwing the ball that you are very serious about receiving the pass.

Less frequently, walk over to your teammate as he or she is picking up the ball and **tell them exactly what you plan to do**. This does not work as well when your team is behind because it takes time off the clock to communicate with them. At the very least, this will draw considerable pressure towards you because the opposition will think you will be the player receiving the ball. As a result, you will potentially create a situation where another teammate is poorly covered or open entirely. Taking pressure away from other players on your team may not be tracked directly on the stat sheet, but it will surely help your team score a few more goals over the course of a season.

In addition, **consider having a few set plays that your team organizes for a game.** First, have a set play where someone is 5 or so yards in front of the person taking the throw-in and have none of your teammates behind them. Then, as the throw-in is being taken, have a person run in behind that person, so the thrower may throw it further down the field. This play often creates a considerable amount of space behind the defense. Otherwise, another set play is a simple 1-2. Start 5-7 yards away from the teammate taking the throw-in and by gesturing with your hands, show him or her a 1 and then a 2 using your fingers. This will indicate to him or her that you are preparing to pass the ball back with only one touch as soon as they play the ball to you. They will have a better view of the field since they likely just scanned it to see who was open before they took the throw-in.

In conclusion, when you are the person taking the throw-in, play the ball to a teammate's foot when there are no defenders between you and them. Avoid high-pressure spots on the field when throwing the ball in. Consider playing the ball backward only if you have an open and trustworthy defender. Also, consider using a fake to fool the other team. When you want the teammate taking the throw-in to pass you the ball, run into space so that you can more easily attack up the field. Potentially, walk over to your teammate and tell him or her exactly what you want to happen. Furthermore, have a set play or two for your team to increase the chances of not only maintaining possession of the ball during a throw-in but quickly advancing up the field on this set piece.

Chapter 17

One-Touch and Wall Passing

Do not be afraid of one-touch passing. Often players have one of two beliefs that reduce their desire to perform one-touch passing. First, if you pass the ball as soon as you receive it, you no longer have an opportunity to make an impact for your team. Obviously, this is far from the truth. A great soccer player looks for the best situations for their team to succeed, which will often be situations where the individual succeeds. Secondly, a much more common reason that **soccer players are uncomfortable with using a one-touch pass is because they are afraid they will mess up**. Sure, that may happen, but the best way to become better at something is to practice it. The same goes for one-touch passing.

Be sure to follow through with your passing leg to increase the accuracy. Consider passing 12 inches in the air for passes that are 7 yards or more to ensure that passes go over a defender's outstretched leg and also has minimal friction from rolling on the ground. **One-touch passing speeds the pace of play up. Though, for many players, it increases the chance of an inaccurate pass since you did not take a first touch to control the ball.**

Wall Pass (1-2 Pass)

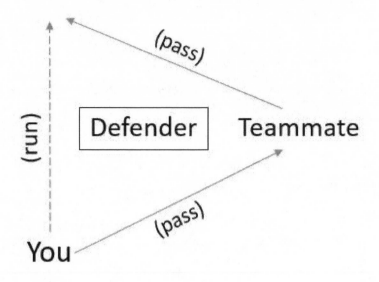

Consider a wall pass, which is also known as a 1-2 pass. **A wall pass is when you pass it to a teammate and they pass it back to you with one touch, similar to if you were to pass a ball against a wall.** Wall passing helps to reduce your worry of not receiving the ball back. Additionally, wall passes are most often done when you are 5-10 yards from a teammate, which increases your chance for accuracy too! Avoid long distance wall passing as it increases your chances to mess up. Wall passing is best done around a single defender. Allow the ball to do a significant amount of the work instead of you trying to use a foot skill to beat a defender. When possible keep your wall passes on the ground. Though some professionals can successfully wall pass the ball in the air, this again increases your chances for mistakes that lead to the other team stealing possession of the ball.

If you are the person starting the wall pass, you must explode after making your initial pass to your teammate. An explosive run indicates you want the ball back and will create separation between you and the defender. However, wall passes can occur when neither you nor the person you pass the ball to move, but it will not help you move the ball around a defender this way. **Keep in mind that if your teammate makes several runs for you and you never reward them with the ball, do not expect them to keep making runs for you.**

An example of a player who is known for his passing, including his wall passing, is Xavi. Xavi was a player on the Spanish National Team which had outstanding successes in 2008, 2010, and in 2012. Additionally, he was a player on the Barcelona team that won the 2014-2015 Champions League final. He was always looking for open space to travel into after his initial pass of the wall pass. He averaged 100 passes or so per game and became known for his effectiveness in passing around defenders and the positive impact he had on his team.

In summary, if you are the person starting a wall pass, you have to pass effectively and receive the pass efficiently. Perform wall passes when you are close to a teammate and use one-touch passing in a wall pass to make it quicker. Accurate one-touch passing is beneficial and can be significantly improved when practiced. To increase repetitions with it, try emphasizing it in practices, where mistakes are not as costly as they would be in a game. Also, practicing by using a real wall, you will improve your explosiveness and reflexes by hurrying to receive quick rebounds off the wall.

Conclusion

The main thing is to keep the main thing the main thing. This statement is so true in life and in soccer. In soccer, the main thing to keep in mind is to develop the abilities that you are most likely to use on the field, without spending much time on those things that would only be used occasionally. Referring back to the preface of this book, the Individual's Pyramid of Importance concept is an excellent indicator of which topics in soccer to emphasize and how your practice time should be spent. For this book specifically, keep in mind that most of your time should be spent on the basic skills of passing with the inside of your foot, taking an attacking touch when receiving the ball, working on weighting your passes, and looking at pressure before you receive a pass.

This book and the other books in the series are meant to be read and understood, but also act as a guide to which you can refer back. Therefore, do not be afraid after you are done with this book, to open it from time to time to get a refresher on the tips, tricks, tweaks, and techniques for improving your abilities. **Keep in mind that a soccer player who wants to take their game to the next level will do what it takes to find the information that will help take him or her there.** Then, he or she will implement the information in practice to ensure it can be used in a game. The process of reading about how to become better, focusing on improving in practice, and then playing better in a game provides for continued growth and progress in any soccer player's career. However, be skeptical about some of the people creating YouTube videos. Many of the "soccer experts" that I have recently found on YouTube are showing poor form. The poor form results from people with little experience actually using the skills themselves in a game. This book provides a great opportunity to read the words and gain the understandings needed to grow. Keep working to be the best player that you can be and I look forward to talking with you in the next book in the series.

If you enjoyed this book, please leave me a review on Amazon letting me know what you enjoyed.

Bonus!

Wouldn't it be nice to have the steps in this book on an easy 3-page printout for you to take to the field? Well, here is your chance!

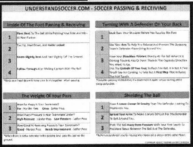

Go to this Link for an **Instant** 3-Page Printout:
UnderstandSoccer.com/free-printout

This FREE guide is simply a "Thank You" for purchasing this book. This 3-page printout will ensure that the knowledge you obtain from this book makes it to the field.

Free Book?

How would you like to obtain the next book in the series for free and have it before anyone else?

Join the Soccer Squad Book Team today and receive your next book (and potentially future books) for FREE.

Signing up is easy and does not cost anything.

Check out this website for more information:

understandsoccer.com/soccer-squad-book-team

Thank You for Reading!

Dear Reader,

I hope you enjoyed and learned from the **Soccer Scoring Bundle**. I truly enjoyed writing these steps and tips to ensure you improve your game, your team's game, or your child's game.

While I was writing these books and having others critique them, I received some great insights. As an author, I love feedback. Honestly, you are the reason that I wrote these books and plan to write more. Therefore, tell me what you liked, what you loved, what can be improved, and even what you hated. I'd love to hear from you. Visit UnderstandSoccer.com and scroll to the bottom of the homepage to leave me a message in the contact section or email me at Dylan@UnderstandSoccer.com.

Finally, I need to ask a favor. I'd love and truly appreciate a review of **Soccer Scoring Bundle**.

Reviews are a key part of the process to determine whether you, the reader, enjoyed the books. The reviews allow me to write more books and to continue to write articles on the UnderstandSoccer.com website. You have the power to help improve my book. Please take the 2 minutes needed to leave a review on Amazon.com at https://www.amazon.com/gp/product-review/1949511065.

Thank you so much for reading the **Soccer Scoring Bundle** and for spending time with me to help improve your game.

In gratitude,

Dylan Joseph

Glossary

50-50 - When a ball is passed into pressure or cleared up the field and your teammate and a player on the opposing team each have an equal (50%) chance of taking possession of the soccer ball.

Attacking Touch - Pushing the ball into space with your first touch, which is the opposite of taking a touch where the ball stops underneath you (at your feet).

Ball Hawk - Someone usually close to the ball, in the right place at the right time, and a person who specializes in scoring rebounds.

Bat - The bone (hardest portion) of your foot.

Bent/Curved Shot - A shot that spins and curves as it goes towards the net. This shot is used when you need to shoot around defenders or goalkeepers. Though you use the bone of your foot to strike the ball instead of following through the ball with your entire body, you just follow through with your leg and cross your legs after shooting the ball.

Bicycle Kick ("Overhead Kick") - where the ball is above you and you proceed to jump up and kick the ball over your body while the ball is in the air.

Broom - In this book, it is the area on your foot towards your toes. There is space in your shoe between your toes where there is a lot more fabric and a lot less bone, which makes it a soft area on your foot, similar to the softness of a broom.

Champions League - The UEFA Champions League is an annual soccer competition involving the best of the best club teams from many of the professional leagues in Europe.

Chop - This is performed with the outside of your foot. The leg that is cutting the ball must step entirely past the ball.

Then, allow the ball to hit that leg/foot, which effectively stops the ball. Having the ball stop next to your foot enables the ball to be pushed in a different direction quickly.

Counterattack ("Fast Break") - When the team defending gains possession of the ball and quickly travels up the field with the objective of taking a quick shot, so few of the other team's players can travel back to defend in time.

Crossbar Challenge - Played by one or more people where you attempt to hit the crossbar by shooting the ball from the 18-yard box.

Cruyff - Cut the ball, but leave yourself between the defender and the ball. In essence, you are cutting the ball behind your plant leg.

Cut - This is performed with the inside of your foot. The leg that is cutting the ball must step entirely past the ball. Then, allow the ball to hit that leg/foot, which effectively stops the ball. Having the ball stop next to your foot enables the ball to be pushed in a different direction quickly. Additionally, you may cut the ball so that it is immediately moving in the direction that you want to go.

Driven Shot - A shot struck with the bone of your foot, where you follow through with your entire body without crossing your legs. This is the most powerful type of shot.

Finishing - The purpose of shooting, which is to score.

Flick - Barely touching the ball to change the direction of the ball slightly for a teammate when a pass is being played to you.

Half-Volley - Striking the ball just after it hit the ground, but while the ball is still in the air.

Jab Step ("Feint," "Body Feint," "Fake," "Fake and Take," or "Shoulder Drop") - When you pretend to push the ball in one direction, but purposely miss, then plant with the foot that you missed the ball with to push the ball in the other direction.

Jockeying - When defending, backpedaling to maintain proper position in relation to the person attacking with the ball. When jockeying, the defender does not dive in for the ball. He or she waits for the ideal time to steal the ball or poke it away.

Jump Turn - Instead of pulling the ball back with the bottom of your foot, as you would do in the V pull back, stop the ball with the bottom of your foot as you jump past the ball, landing with both feet at the same time on the other side of the ball. Landing with both feet at the same time on the other side of the ball allows you to explode away in the direction from which you came.

Offside - When you pass the ball to a player on your team who is past the opposing team's last defender at the moment the kick is initiated. You cannot be offside on a throw-in or when you are on your own half of the field.

One-Time Shot - When a pass or cross is played to you and your first touch is a shot on net.

Opposite Foot - Your non-dominant foot. Out of your two feet, it is the one that you are not as comfortable using.

Outside of the Foot Shot ("Trivela") - Shooting with the bone of your foot where your toe is pointed down and in. The ball makes contact with the outside portion/bone of your foot. This shot is useful because it is quicker than a driven shot, it can provide bend like a bent shot, and is more powerful than a pass shot.

Pass Fake - Faking a pass. Keep your form the same as when you pass, including: 1) Looking at a teammate before you do a pass fake 2) Raise your passing leg high enough behind your body, so that an opponent believes you are going to kick the ball.

Pass Shot ("Finesse Shot") - A shot on the net using the inside of your foot to increase your accuracy. However, land past the ball on the follow through to increase the shot's power, similar to a shot taken with the bone of your foot.

Passing Lane - An area on the field where a teammate can pass you the ball directly, while the ball remains on the ground.

Pitch - A soccer field.

Rainbow - When you place one foot in front of the ball and the laces of the other foot behind the ball. Pin the ball between your feet and flick the ball up behind your body and over your head.

Roll ("Rollover") - Using the bottom of the toes of your foot, roll the ball parallel to the defender, crossing your feet when you plant. Then, bring your other foot around to uncross your feet and push the ball forward. The path the ball takes is the shape of an "L."

Self-Pass ("L," "Iniesta," or "La Croqueta") - Passing the ball from one foot to the other while running. Imagine you are doing a roll, but without your foot going on top of the ball. Instead, it is an inside of the foot pass from one foot and an inside of the foot push up the field with the other foot.

Set Piece ("Dead Ball") - A practiced plan used when the ball goes out of bounds or a foul is committed to put the ball back into play. The most common set pieces are throw-ins and free kicks.

Scissor - When the foot closest to the ball goes around the ball as you are attacking in a game. Emphasize turning your hips to fake the defender. To easily turn your hips, plant past the ball with your foot that is not going around the ball so that you can use the momentum of the moving ball to your advantage.

Shielding - Placing your body between the ball and the defender. With your back facing the defender and your arms wide, prevent him or her from traveling to the ball.

Shot Fake - Faking a shot. Make sure your form looks the same as when you shoot, including: 1) Looking at the goal before you do a shot fake 2) Arms out 3) Raise your shooting leg high enough behind your body, so it looks like you are going to shoot.

Square to your Teammate - Pointing your hips at a teammate.

Step On Step Out - In order to change direction, step on the ball with the bottom of your foot. Then, with the same foot that stepped on the ball, take another step to plant to the side of the ball, so that your other leg can come through and push the ball in a different direction.

Step Over - When you are next to the ball and you have your furthest leg from the ball step over the ball, so your entire body turns as if you are going in a completely different direction. The step over is best used along a sideline.

Through Ball/Run - When a pass is played into space in front of you, allowing you to continue your forward momentum.

Toe Poke/Toe Blow - Striking the ball with your big toe. The toe poke is the quickest shot, but often the most inaccurate shot.

Upper 90 - Either of the top corners on a net (corners are 90 degrees).

V Pull Back - Pull the ball backward using the bottom of your foot. Then, use your other leg to push the ball and accelerate forward in the other direction, hence the "V" in the V pull back.

Volley - Striking the ball out of the air before it hits the ground.

Wall Passing ("1-2 Passing") - A wall pass is when you pass it to a teammate and they pass it back to you with one touch similar to if you were to pass a ball against a wall.

Acknowledgments

I would like to thank you, the reader. I am grateful to provide you value and to help you on your journey of becoming a more confident soccer player, coach, or parent. I am happy to serve you and thank you for the opportunity to do so. Also, I would like to recognize people that have made a difference and have paved the way for me to share this book with you:

First, I want to thank my mother who has been a role model for what can be done when you work hard towards your goals. Her work ethic and ability to overcome adversity are truly admirable, and I look up to her for this. Also, I appreciate her feedback on wording and grammatical improvements.

Second, I would like to thank the editors Kevin Solorio, Kimberly Stewart, Paul Marvar, Tom Catalano, Toni Sinistaj, and Youssef Hodroj. They reviewed this book for areas that could be improved and additional insights to share. Without their input, this book would not be the high-quality reading material you have come to expect in the Understand Soccer Series.

Lastly, I would like to thank my soccer trainer, Aaron Byrd, whose wisdom and smarts have turned me into the player I am today. His guidance and knowledge about this game have made it so that I can pass this knowledge on to rising stars, coaches looking to grow their understanding of soccer, and caring parents!

Many thanks,

Dylan Joseph

What's Next?

Each of the chapters in this book aims to increase your ability to dribble past the other team. Implementing the tips, tricks, tweaks, and techniques you just read in this book will surely help you in achieving your dreams to become an outstanding soccer player. If you enjoyed the contents of this book, please visit my website at UnderstandSoccer.com to let me know what you were most excited to read.

I aim to create a book on topics covered in the first book in the series *Soccer Training: A Step-by-Step Guide on 14 Topics for Intelligent Soccer Players, Coaches, and Parents* and would love for you to answer the **one question poll** at UnderstandSoccer.com/poll to help me determine what area of soccer you want to improve next. The fourth book in the series will be *Soccer Passing & Receiving: A Step-by-Step Guide on How to Work with Your Teammates.* However, your vote on the upcoming books in the series will help determine what book is to follow!

35414238R00183

Made in the USA
San Bernardino, CA
10 May 2019